Etiquette for the Average Joe
Volume II

by

Martin Stuart

authorHOUSE™

1663 LIBERTY DRIVE, SUITE 200
BLOOMINGTON, INDIANA 47403
(800) 839-8640
WWW.AUTHORHOUSE.COM

First published by AuthorHouse 09/27/04

ISBN: 1-4184-8926-3 (sc)

Printed in the United States of America
Bloomington, Indiana

This book is printed on acid-free paper.

Acknowledgments

To my illustrator, Ron Therien, who so wonderfully adds animation to my ideas, to Tamar Love, my editor, who adds delightful magic of her own, to Kathy and John Homuth, John Moffet and the friends throughout my life, to my family, who gives me courage, to my nieces and nephews, who light up my life from LA to Indiana, and to my wife, who has given me her heart, her soul and her smile.

Table of Contents

Introduction

Etiquette, as I have learned, is a never-ending subject. I wish I could tell you this book is about etiquette at weddings or etiquette on a golf course, but this book is a guide to everyday life. Yes, we need such a guide: many people don't know the difference between good manners or bad, simple as the distinction might be. As long as we live, people will display bad manners on a daily basis...which will only give me the material I need to keep writing.

Etiquette is really not a difficult concept to grasp—as long as you're a willing participant. I'm no genius; I'm just the guy who decided to point out these little things. I'm here to help; give me a little of your time, and, together, we will make miracles happen.

Maybe you're the kind of guy who doesn't want to be told what he's doing wrong. Fine, but you're upsetting many people as you drive the freeway every day with a finger up your nose. Here's a quick etiquette tip: don't pick in public. Was that so difficult?

Similarly, if you're stuck in an elevator, you may think it's funny if you have gas, but it sure won't be any laughing matter for your fellow passengers. Use your brain and remember the rules of etiquette, Stinky, and you won't get the stink-eye en route to the 14th floor.

When you start slipping back into your bad manners, pick up this book for a quick refresher. If you don't like to read, I've included cartoons in every chapter. If you don't like cartoons, then send me an email. If you're not connected to the Internet, then I can always send smoke signals.

Glad to have you back,

MARTIN STUART

All Hands

Just last month, one of my closest friends came over for dinner. I hadn't seen him in a while, so I didn't know what to expect in the area of table manners. Unfortunately, his hands came into contact with the meal more than his mouth did. When he told me that he rarely used his knife, but instead preferred to use his forefinger to coax food onto his fork, I knew I was in for a long night.

I know I've already touched on the subject of using fingers to shovel food—either into your mouth or onto your fork—but it bears repeating: your hand is not an eating utensil. Please, do not use it as one.

Hoping to lead by gentle example, I decided to take my friend who eats like an ape out for dinner. I told my friend that I witnessed poor eating habits on a daily basis and did nothing about it but cringe, but because he was a friend, I felt an obligation to turn him around. It was up to him to use this information or disregard it.

We covered the basics: holding a fork and knife and knowing when to use them, placing a napkin on your lap, refraining from chewing ice from your water glass and waiting to begin eating until everyone has their meal.

He absorbed the information I gave him, giving me hope he'd remember it beyond this introductory dinner lesson. Whether he wants to eat with his hands from here on out is entirely up to him. Now, at least, he has the knowledge to better himself...if he wants.

Bachelor Party

So you're throwing your brother a bachelor party in Las Vegas. You have it all set up: hotel accommodations, restaurants and live entertainment. As it turns out, you have other friends planning to be in Las Vegas at that time, so after the bachelor festivities, you're hoping to spend some quality time with them, as well.

Hold the phone, Mr. Party Planner—this is your brother we're talking about! If he's lucky, this will be on the only bachelor party ever thrown in his honor. Even if it isn't your brother, but a close friend, you still have a responsibility to be there with him, not with other friends who may be in town.

You'll have plenty of other chances to visit Sin City, so keep the bachelor party weekend focused on the guy who's getting married. This doesn't mean you're banned from seeing anyone else, but know your priorities and try to make any other visits brief and low key. You don't want your brother or other bachelor party attendees to think you have better things to do.

If you are the one who's putting together the bachelor party, set the ground rules before the weekend begins, so there are no surprises when you get there. Take into consideration that some guys may not be able to contribute the same amount of money as others, and work out a budget so you can let each participant know what to expect. Don't object if some folks can't participate in every activity.

During the weekend, take the groom aside from time to time and make sure he's happy. It's his big day, so he should get his heart's desire—within limits!

Bad Habits

Why do men wait until they're on the highway to pick their noses? Is there something about traveling at high speeds that makes this grotesque act seem more acceptable?

Perhaps the freeway has the same effect on nose spelunkers as a baseball field does on players who "feel" the need to check their family jewels in front of a captive audience. Have you ever sat next to that old guy in a deli who sucks the food through his teeth? Ouch! The delicatessen should provide headphones so you can enjoy your meal.

A combination of auditory and visual indecency, spitting is probably the most revolting bad habit to which we are needlessly subjected. If you have to expectorate, try to avoid sidewalks or other common areas. It's bad enough that we're forced to see and hear it; we certainly don't want to step in it.

While on the subject of public places, remember to put trash where it belongs—in a trashcan. Our streets are constantly lined with debris; even at the office, I'll walk into the employee lounge or bathroom and find trash everywhere. It's disgusting and unnecessary.

Each display of public indecency would be avoidable if the guilty party were simply to ask himself, "Would I want to see or hear anyone else do this in public?" If the answer is "No," then keep it to yourself. Bad habits, like dirty laundry, can be quite disgusting, so it's better to leave them at home instead of airing them in public.

Judy's success in entertaining is all about
pizza and placement.

Batting Cleanup

While everyone loves a good party, it's certainly no picnic for the person throwing the bash. Many hosts will hire a catering company to serve food and clean up after their guests; unfortunately, the crowd I run with can barely afford to stock the bar.

If you're lucky enough to be invited to someone's party, do your part as a responsible guest, and pick-up after yourself. Leaving plastic cups or paper plates strewn around the house, tossing trash on the counter—you name it—people love the fact that because it's not their home, they can mess it up.

This kind of mentality may work for a two-year-old, but not a twenty-two year old. How far do you really have to go to find a trashcan?

It really comes down to common courtesy. When you want something to drink, do you leave your old cup wherever you want, knowing quite well you can always find a new one? Would you leave a half-eaten piece of birthday cake atop your television for a week? I don't think so. You would reuse your glass and throw away your cake plate—assuming it is disposable, that is.

I have actually taken a break in the middle of a party to help the host clean up. When I walk around with a big garbage bag, other guys look at me like, "What the heck got into him?"—but least my behavior reminds the other party animals that their trash belongs somewhere other than atop the grand piano.

If the party is winding down, and you're not in a rush, offer to help. Treat the party house like it was your own, with the thought that if you help keep it clean, they may just decide to have another bash...and invite you.

Before You Leave

Once, on an airplane, I sat next to a woman who couldn't stop talking during the flight. Once the plane landed, she got up and left without saying "goodbye." Although her constant yammering had been slightly annoying, I was ready to part with a few kind words, but she was up and out before I had the chance.

I've always found it odd when two people meet and share a connection, but then don't bother to say "goodbye" before they take leave of one another. I guess this might be more of a personal peeve more than any hardcore etiquette rule, but I believe in closure. Even if I'm at a restaurant—assuming I receive good service—I like to thank the waiter or waitress before I leave. It's the courteous thing to do.

Parties are a melting pot, where people meet and never say "goodbye." You spend some time getting to know a good-looking girl, and then her friends show up. She wants to spend a little time with them, and you haven't even had a chance to ask for her phone number. It's up to you, before the night is over, to track her down and see if she would like to hook up in the near future. If you find her in some remote corner of the house, making-out with some other guy, I think it's safe to say she's not interested. Otherwise, for God's sake, get her number! At the very least, say "goodbye." Even if you never see her again, would it kill you to leave her with a good impression?

For goodness sake, say "goodbye" before taking your leave of someone with whom you've spent more than a few minutes talking. It only takes a moment, and who knows? You might form a contact—long-term or short—that makes your day sometime in the future.

Better Put One On

The condom talk is one of the most embarrassing topics to cover, but at the same time, it can save your life. Why sweep condom talk under the table, when you're eventually going to take it out? Make shopping for those little plastic sleeves something the whole family can enjoy...okay, maybe you just want to bring a good friend.

I don't believe shopping for condoms is ranked high on the list of "things to do on a first date." Let's speed up to a few dates later, when you and your sweetheart would like to take the relationship to a new level. Before you get there, why not drop by the local pharmacy to check out the selection?

In Los Angeles, you can visit a boutique store on Melrose Avenue called "Condomania." The Hallmark Gold Crown store of prophylactics, a visit to Condomania is a nice little way to break the ice before the big night. Think about it: You can reach into your bedside table and pull out something that might not work for her physiology, or you can pick out a box together, find something you can both enjoy.

Having the condom talk is a good start toward an open and honest relationship. Because of the myriad assortment of sizes, shapes and colors available, you'll be able to rate one another's honesty quotient. Think about it—you might want to believe that you need the extra-large size, but in due time, she's going to find out the naughty truth. Save yourself some embarrassment, and be honest when you make your selection.

Selecting condoms together may not replace meeting for coffee as the date of choice among singles, but more people really should start "doing it" together (pun intended).

Bill Leaver

Do you know anyone who gets up and walks away right before the restaurant bill arrives? Perhaps he will go outside for a smoke or into the bathroom for an extended stay, but upon his return, Mr. Empty Pockets does not say a word about the bill, behaving as if everything is hunky dory.

If a friend pulls that move on me—even once—it's time to lay the cards on the table and determine just what kind of friend he really is. The best solution is to call him on it immediately, so he'll know never to do it again—at least not in your presence.

On the other side of the table is "Joe Stiff-Ya," who will leave ten dollars for a twenty-dollar meal. He should be handled no differently from his pal, Mr. Empty Pockets. He's not leaving until he pays his fair share—or is made aware of what he owes.

The rule is simple: If you don't have enough money, you don't get to go out to dinner. While it's okay to hit up a good friend for an on-the-spot loan when you find yourself short of change, don't make a habit of it. Just because your friend has money and you don't, it's not his responsibility to bankroll your dinner. However, if you find yourself at a restaurant unexpectedly without funds, let your dining companion know you will pay him back whenever you can.

You might get lucky—your friend might laugh it off and tell you he's not going to hold his breath waiting for you to pay him back—but at least you had the decency to acknowledge your debt and your friend's generosity. Perhaps one day, when you're at a restaurant more conducive to your budget, you can offer to pay for your pal's Grand Slam Breakfast.

"Payroll is a little tight this week, so here's a McDonald's funbook to hold you over."

The Boss Is a Bully

Many of us work for big companies, where we often take for granted receiving health benefits and a weekly paycheck. On the other side of corporate America is the world of the small-business owner. While working for these smaller companies can be fun, it can also be a completely new, sometimes unpleasant, ballgame.

I once worked for a woman who wouldn't pay me until I went into her office and asked for my check. It may have been that she forgot—or maybe it was just her idea of playing "guess who's wearing the boxer shorts"—but her behavior was rude. Anyone who works his tail off all week should not be expected to beg for his pay.

I should be grateful though; other people I know have been completely stiffed by small-business owners. One girl I know helped a man get his accounting practice off the ground, but when she asked for a paycheck a week later, he told her that he could not pay her. Revolting.

Any time an employee has to ask his boss what's going on with the finances, it's time to start looking for a new gig. People love power, and many of these individuals who call themselves "the boss" will be extremely sweet to get you to work for them, but once you're there, it's like Jekyll and Hyde.

Once you witness this behavioral change, don't put up with it any longer than necessary. That doesn't mean you should quit, but if something better comes along, then by all means give your two-week's notice and don't look back.

On the other hand, if your boss sits you down and tells you it's going to be a rocky road for a while, give him or her a chance, as long as it's a job you enjoy. Many people became rich because they stuck it out through tough times. As long as your boss communicates with you and listens to what you have to say, then it may be well worth the wait.

"I forgot to mention, they're very strict
about using prongs."

Buffet Buffoon

You're standing at the salad bar, using the prongs to lift a cherry tomato, when the guy next to you gets restless and begins picking at the cucumbers with his bare hands. Coughing and sneezing around the food is simply intolerable, even when a sneeze guard is present. So much for the sanitary salad-bar experience—it's time to drop your plate and order from the menu.

Buffets are a serious danger zone, where more than one person I know has been subjected to food poisoning. Most buffets go way beyond salad; therefore you see people grabbing everything from shrimp to strips of bacon. I have even witnessed a woman doing a taste test of the salad dressings, using nothing more than her index finger. I was tempted to give her the finger in return...

Unfortunately, some people will not learn until they're told. If someone next to you is popping croutons in his mouth to kill time, kindly let him know you were planning to take croutons from the same bowl and would appreciate if he were to use a utensil instead of his hands. Try to kill these offenders with kindness, as opposed to starting an all-out food fight.

People are entitled to do what they want in the privacy of their own homes, but as far as I'm concerned, if my meal is coming from the same place as theirs, they need to learn how to be considerate of others. Buffets can be fun, as long as the people in line are safe and sanitary with the food that's being served.

Building a Foundation

If you've ever had a chance to visit Grand Canyon, you saw it was made of thousands of layers, which helped build up the canyon over many centuries. Layers are also important in building a relationship—in which they are more commonly known as a "foundation"—and a strong one is essential for any lasting monument.

Here's an example of a relationship that went south because of a weak foundation: My friend, Abigail, met a guy she slept with immediately for two weeks straight. Then, one night, he went home and never called her again. Her heart was broken, but outside of the sex, the two of them didn't really know anything about one another. They had no foundation on which to build any sort of relationship.

If a relationship is what you're looking for, sex shouldn't come into play until you've had time to build a solid, friendly foundation. While sex might seem more fun, foundation building can foster some of the greatest moments in your relationship. Try taking long walks, going to see films, talking on the phone, going out for dinner, meeting for a drink or even cooking a meal together. (Note: I didn't suggest getting together with friends because you should get to know her before a third party is brought into the equation.)

It may be difficult to understand how going to a movie can build a relationship's foundation, but if you think about it, you'll see it makes sense. You can share a tub of popcorn, laugh together during a good comedy, sigh or groan at a weighty art film and bond over a drink or a meal afterwards. The point of the activity is to get to know each other better, to find out if there's anything more substantial to your relationship than pure passion.

Busboy Strike!

Everybody loves to get out of the house and go to a restaurant, but little things always creep up, things you need to be aware of if you are going to dine happily.

In the first volume of *Etiquette for the Average Joe,* I touched upon the importance of a good restaurant's letter grade, as well as the importance of the freshness of the food it serves. I also talked about dirty floors, so it's only appropriate that I now discuss dirty dishes, which you should only see at the *end* of your meal.

I'm not talking about a dirty glass here or a spotty fork there; I'm talking about numerous tables stacked with dirty dishes. One Sunday afternoon, when a friend and I went out for lunch, our first thought was that there must have been a busboy strike. It didn't matter which direction we turned—the restaurant was filled with tables that had not been cleared off. If you are capable of enjoying a meal in such surroundings, I applaud you. As for me, one look was all it took for us to get the heck out of there.

If you're lucky enough to avoid a busboy strike, keep an eye out for the level of cleanliness the restaurateurs bring to the table. For example, I witnessed a busboy wipe a table with a wet rag, and then bring me a glass of water. Unfortunately, the hand he wiped the table with was now touching the top of the glass from which I was about to drink. Ugh.

It may look silly, especially if you're on a date, but I always ask for a straw so I don't have to put my lips where any waiter or busboy may have put his dirty hands. Call me paranoid, but if my choices are suffering from food poisoning, catching the *ebola* virus or using a straw, I'll take the straw!

Buying In Bulk

Don't you hate spending nearly two dollars for a roll of paper towels at a supermarket and then finding the same roll at a discount store for under a buck? Welcome to the world of Smart & Final, Costco and Sam's Club.

Joe and Jane Consumer, tired of having to rely on double coupons, are now shopping at warehouse stores, which offer deep savings without coupons. The secret? More often than not, the stores require you to buy in bulk, rather than one item at a time.

For instance, you may have to buy a four-pack of toothpaste or a case of soda, instead of buying one tube or one six-pack. You may not want a case of soda, but you will most likely wind up drinking it, and in the end, your savings will negate any annoyance you might feel at the cans of sodas taking up valuable real estate in your refrigerator.

Mind you, every now and then supermarkets offer great deals on household staples. When they do, buy in bulk, because it may be a while until they advertise that price again. Just make sure you have enough storage space—your guests shouldn't be subjected to sharing your sofa with a 12-pound box of Tide.

Other viable options are stores like K-Mart, Target and Wal-Mart, where you'll find a single toothbrush at a lower price than at most supermarkets. You'll battle extended families with screaming children for your place in line, but you won't pay an annual membership fee or get stuck buying four toothbrushes when you only want one.

No matter where you shop, be aware that you don't have to be at the mercy of supermarket prices. There are plenty of cheaper options from which you can choose. Don't be afraid to buy in bulk, and always be on the lookout for the best possible savings.

Calling From Your Car

While cell phones are a nice luxury, they can also pose a serious danger to you and those around you. If you're behind the wheel, all it takes is a split second for a major accident to occur. Calling the local deli to place your lunch order is important, but it's going to be tough to digest your sandwich if your head is rolling around on the freeway.

If you still feel the need to talk while you're driving, get a hands-free set so that your main focus remains the highway. Furthermore, don't complicate matters by trying to eat while you're on the phone AND driving. Munching on some kosher pickles is an unpleasant sound the person on the other end can do without, as is the five-car accident you're sure to cause if you attempt this circus act.

People are caught up trying to do many different things behind the wheel, including changing CDs, putting on makeup and checking out the other beautiful people on the road. In essence, they forget to do what they are supposed to do in the first place: drive.

If you feel that talking on the phone does not affect your driving, you're out of your mind. I'm a hardheaded fool, just like you, but I also consider myself a good driver. I thank my lucky stars that I'm alive today and have not injured anyone by all the senseless errors I've made behind the wheel while talking on the phone.

Keep your eyes on the road and avoid using the phone—or doing anything else!—unless it's a real emergency, such as an accident. Unless it's completely necessary, put the phone down and give it a rest. All the other drivers will be happy you did.

Cancel and You're Dead

Two weeks ago, you set a date with Bonnie—it's been difficult getting together because of your conflicting schedules—and you've spoken with her a few times since. Finally, the day arrives when you're going to see her, but there's one problem: While you've been waiting for your date, you've met someone else. Do you call Bonnie to cancel, or do you act like a gentleman and keep the date?

The answer is B, act like a gentleman. First of all, if you've just met someone, it's too early to figure out whether or not it's going to work. Second, Bonnie cleared her calendar to make room for you, so don't leave her hanging. You don't have to ask her to marry you; just have a nice time and enjoy your evening together. You made a commitment. Keep it.

Sometimes dates are scheduled weeks in advance, but then, when the date draws closer, your enthusiasm has diminished. It doesn't necessarily have to be a date with a woman; it could simply be a party or a ballgame that you and your buddies were planning to attend. When you made the plans, you thought they sounded good. Now, you've changed your mind. It happens all the time.

If you make plans, don't think about canceling unless it's an emergency. It doesn't reflect well on you, and it certainly doesn't help while trying to maintain friendships. Your friends will just get tired of making plans with you, knowing that you'll probably have some lame, last-minute excuse for why you can't go.

Allow me to speak from experience. Just about every time I've bailed out on an event, I've ended up regretting it. Do yourself a favor, go out and have a great time. Life is too short to stay home.

Candle in the Wind

I recently went to blow out a candle and was almost blinded by the backdraft: a spark nearly caught me in the eye. Luckily, I wasn't hurt, but the experience taught me to find out the correct way to blow out candles.

My mother owned a candlesnuffer, which she constantly told me to use. Imagine a young, growing boy having to choose between using a candlesnuffer and blowing out the candles. Naturally, I went with using my mouth to blow out the candles—and then my mother would curse me as she tried to get the wax off the formal dining-room table.

A candlesnuffer is always a safe bet, but because most men are lazy, twenty snuffers may be available, and we'll still use our mouths or even our fingers. If you must blow, put your palm up near the edge of the candle and blow at an angle. As long as the candle isn't on a surface that can be damaged with wax spillage, then you're okay.

On a "lighter" note, candles are an inexpensive but elegant way to impress a woman. You can live in a beat-up old apartment, but light a candle and you're instantly creating a brand-new atmosphere. It also makes it more difficult for her to see what kind of shape the place is really in...

Candles with fragrance not only are sensual, but also help eliminate bad odors that may be lingering around your pad. Pick up a fragrant candle at any supermarket or local drug store, and it will soon light up your night—and many more nights to come!

Career Confusion

How many people are genuinely happy with what they do for a living? Living in Los Angeles, I see hundreds of struggling actors doing everything from waiting tables to just plain waiting.

Engineers want to be managers, managers want to be vice-presidents and vice-presidents want to be CEO. Of course, there are thousands of unemployed people who would be happy just to find a job...

If you are unhappy with whatever you are doing, start looking into other job possibilities. If there's something in your heart that you really want to do, don't cheat yourself—go out and show the world how well you can do it. If you haven't a clue of what you want to do, try to find an entry-level job at a company you really like. If you work hard and keep your eyes open to possibilities, you'll find your niche.

You don't want to give notice until you find something better, so keep your job hunt low-key, and don't let anyone at your current job know about it. Think twice about whom you tell—one slip of the tongue could jeopardize your future at the company, even if you only plan for that future to be a few more months in length.

Change is good, as is taking a risk or two. My brother-in-law moved up the ranks of a company, but reached a point where they would not promote him any further. He decided to break out on his own, and admits it was the scariest thing he's ever done. Six years later, I strive to be as successful as him.

Don't ever let your dreams die. To quote the great Sally Weston from her bestselling autobiography, *My Life in the Sky*, "No matter where you're from, no matter who people think you are, you can be whatever you want."

Cheating Heart

One of two things can happen if you cheat: Either you will enjoy it and begin to cheat more often, or you will realize that no other woman compares to the one with whom you are currently partnered.

If you're a guy who wants to cheat on his wife or girlfriend, there's not much I can say or do to stop you. Cheating is not something I encourage, but sometimes getting it out of your system is the only thing to do. Some men talk about cheating but never do it, carrying around their unrequited cheating hearts and never completely losing the urge to explore, making themselves and their partners miserable.

Everyone has a fantasy, and while it usually features someone besides your partner, it doesn't mean you have to cheat to make your dream come true. There's no need to venture elsewhere until you give your woman the opportunity to make you happy, and she can't do that until you tell her what you want.

If you open up to your woman about your fantasies, you might be surprised at what happens. Some men are content with a magazine or a video; a good friend's wife happens to enjoy watching videos with him—yes, his friends are jealous of his good fortune!

Women like it hot and wild as much as men, but men have a tendency to "close down" emotionally after being with a woman for a while. That's the first thing you have to correct. Open up, gentlemen, and let your woman inside.

Once you start to communicate, you may still feel the urge to merge with another. If that's the case, lay it on the line with the woman with whom you were once in love. Don't drag her through your illicit escapades. Be a man and end the relationship in a respectful way—it's the least she deserves.

To deter double-dipping, Linda cuts her vegetables into one-inch pieces.

Chip & Dip

My friend, Dave, and I played a round of golf, and then settled into the clubhouse for a cold drink. The waitress brought us a basket of chips on which to munch while we were waiting for our lunch order to arrive, and I groaned—I knew what was coming next.

Dave is a heck of a golfer, but he doesn't know the first thing about eating chips. He often takes a chip, looks at it, and, if he doesn't like the looks of that particular chip, throws it back in the basket, basically saying, "This chip is not good enough for me, but you might like it!"

I told Dave to hell with him. If he's going to touch the chip, it's his. He could do whatever he wants with it at that point...I don't care. Take it home, sell it at a swap meet, feed it to the birds, but don't put it back in the same basket from which I'm eating!

I guess re-basketing chips falls under the same category as double dipping: both are a big no-no. For a fresh bowl of chips and dip, you're only allowed one dip per chip. Likewise, if you pick up a chip, it's no longer community property—it's yours. If you happen to arrive at a party and find more chips in the dip bowl than there is dip itself, you might want to move on to the vegetable platter!

These are the rules: Like them or not, if you want to eat chips and dip, you'd better follow them. If you think the rules are a bit harsh, let me offer a simple suggestion; find a small cup and pour some dip into that cup so you can dive into your private reserve as often as you like. Let this rule of thumb carry over into the world of vegetables and finger sandwiches, too. Act like a gentleman; eat like a gentleman.

Christmas-Card Madness

What a year it's been! You got married and bought a house and, for your first Christmas together, your wife wants to put a picture of the two of you on your holiday cards.

Don't worry. When faced with Christmas-card madness, it's natural to consider divorce or even an annulment, but, as most married men learn, it's best to relax and let your wife do whatever makes her happy. You'll be pleasantly surprised at the results.

As a single guy, I didn't usually send out cards. I would simply pick up the phone and wish my family and friends a happy holiday. Then, one year, I must have made a small donation to the Humane Society and the American Heart Association because they both sent me about twenty blank holiday cards in late October. I figured greeting cards cost about three dollars each and I had twenty for a ten-dollar donation. What a deal! These were not the most exotic cards, but family, friends and work associates were stunned to receive something from me in the mail, making the whole production quite worthwhile.

If you happen to receive a card from someone who wasn't on your recipient list, make sure to get one out as soon as possible in return, otherwise your pal will know he didn't make the holiday-card A-list. You might also give your pal a call to acknowledge how much you appreciated his card.

As you get older, people expect a little more from you, and a holiday card is a small sacrifice to let other people know you care...especially if you're fortunate enough to get a few for free.

Stan got tired of trying to remember what
side to walk on, so Hazel and he agreed
to go through life single file.

Close to the Curb

It may be old-fashioned, sexist and nearly forgotten, but in my book, the rule still stands: If you and a woman are walking down the street, the man should always be closest to the curb.

Many women aren't aware of this rule, so if you're on a date and make a sudden move toward the street, you might want to explain that you are simply demonstrating proper etiquette and not searching the gutter for loose change.

The same holds true if you go shopping together. The least you can do is offer to carry a few bags so she isn't stuck hauling everything. Even if it's one bag, it may look a little odd if she is carrying a load and you're carrying nothing.

There's more to taking a walk with a woman than meets the eye. I was with my wife, Beckie, the other night, and she didn't know why I wouldn't hold her hand. It's not that I didn't want to, I explained. It's just that I hadn't thought about it...my fault, I suppose. She is happiest though, when I'm walking closest to the curb and holding her hand. Beckie probably thinks like most women and would want her man to do the same. You make the call.

Etiquette has its limits. If your date expects you to throw down your jacket over a puddle so she doesn't get her feet wet, tell her you know a good detour only a block away. As long as I've been practicing proper etiquette, I have never had to remove any article of clothing to cover a puddle. To me, that's very "old school," and with today's dry-cleaning costs, I'll carry her over that puddle before I take off my clothes.

Nobody wants to share an office with
"Coffee Grind Carl," not even
the cleaning crew.

Coffee Grinds & Nicotine

A work associate stopped by my desk to drop off some paperwork. It was relatively early, a time when most people were enjoying a cup of coffee or two so their bodies could kick into gear. This employee, who I will refer to as "Coffee-Grind Carl," brought with him a smell of coffee and nicotine so foul that I had to wonder if there was such a thing as third-hand smoke. I was still smelling ol' "Coffee Grind" long after he walked away.

Trends are strange...that when certain fashions go out of style, people have no problem getting rid of their old clothes. Now that smoking is no longer in style, plenty of people who still haven't quit, health risks be damned.

If you're a smoker, don't be like Carl who smokes a carton a day. Have a few cigarettes, if you must, but try to limit your intake of tobacco. If you're still smoking, even with the number of anti-smoking campaigns, please understand that many people you work with have quit for good reason and don't need to be reminded of what they gave up. In other words, after you smoke, pop a mint and allow your fresh, fragrant tobacco breath to settle before you return to the office.

Coffee really isn't good for you, either. Considering bad breath, discolored teeth and the cost of a cup of Joe, coffee and cigarettes might just bankrupt you before they kill you.

I emailed an article to a close friend about how smoking claimed five-thousand lives in 2001. It's an incredibly sensitive issue with all smokers, but I care for my friend, and I don't want him to die. If you know someone like "Coffee-Grind Carl," don't threaten him by saying that he'd better quit. Instead, support the possibility of him doing so. It's better than not saying anything at all.

Diamonds Are a Man's Best Friend

The minority of professional athletes these days are those who walk around with less than a pound of jewelry on them. Some of these guys have more gold than Fort Knox! If that's not enough, they're also wearing more diamonds than any woman I know. How these guys get through airport security is a mystery to me, but if that's the look they like, then all the more power to them.

Nowadays, men are experimenting in treatments that were once strictly a woman's purview. Manicures, pedicures and facials are now part of a weekly routine for many men. I used to bite my fingernails, which was a pretty disgusting habit. I finally tried a manicure and haven't taken a bite since. I did try a clear polish on my nails once, and quickly realized it's not the best look for me. The point is that there is no harm in making yourself look good, but there is a limit as to how far you should go.

Professional athletes are constantly in the spotlight, so they have that "larger than life" image to which they must live up. Hence, they can get away with flashy jewelry and maybe even flashy fingernails, but for guys like you and me, it's better to keep our image low key.

These athletes are gods in the eyes of many men who try to dress like them. Unfortunately, that gold-plated necklace and those cubic zirconium earrings are not going to measure up to what the big boys are wearing. If the jewelry doesn't measure up, there's a good chance the person wearing them won't, either. On the other hand, if you dress within in your means, I can already tell you're going to be a superstar.

"Hi, my name is Rex. How am I
doing so far?"

Don't Be a Spaz

It happens all the time: A guy sees an unbelievable-looking girl, walks up and says the first lame thing that comes to him, without giving it too much thought. Nine times out of ten, that guy is going to sound like a spaz, and the gorgeous girl will take a walk.

Because women are hit on more than tennis balls, they're often just waiting to shoot down the next idiot who gets in their faces. However, if you're not too pushy and don't come off as too eager—like a caveman about to clobber his woman over the head and drag her back to his cave—you might stand a chance.

Guys think that by flashing car keys and fancy jewelry, they're actually making progress. If that's the case, what quality of woman are we actually talking about? If she's only after the bling bling, is she really worth your time? Instead of being too eager, take a step back, relax and evaluate the situation. A basketball player doesn't go into a game without warming up, so why should you?

In the first volume of *Etiquette for the Average Joe,* I wrote a chapter entitled "Less Is More." There's a lot of truth to that homily, so instead of opening with how much you make, tone it down to a simple "hello." Make eye contact, give her a smile and speak from the heart. It doesn't matter if you're in a bar and comment on how poorly the air conditioner is—at least you're being honest about something to which you can both relate. Remember, she may be a supermodel, but she's not a superhuman being.

If you want to follow up your "hello" with a quote from your stock portfolio, go ahead. At least you showed sincerity from the start, and you didn't come off as a total spaz…at least not yet.

Don't Keep 'Em Waiting

The job interview is set for 2:00 p.m. and you show up at 1:45, just to be safe. One hour later, you start to wonder what could be taking so long. Two hours later, you're about to throw in the towel.

People in the position of job authority think they can throw their weight around and begin the interview whenever they want. Don't be a moron. If you are conducting the interview, don't keep your guest waiting any longer than necessary. Treat the interviewee with respect, and keep him posted if you are running behind schedule.

The same is true for any kind of meeting. You set a time for a reason, so honor your appointments and be prompt. If, for some reason of emergency, you must be late, then use the phone. A quick call will do wonders to keep your professional reputation intact.

The same is true for non-work-related appointments. I recently visited a close friend I hadn't seen in a while. Immediately after entering the house, I was directed to sit in the living room, alone, for thirty minutes, while she gabbed endlessly on the phone. I could not believe what nerve this person had, treating me like a non-entity.

If you have guests, it's better to avoid answering the phone altogether, but if you must, inform your guests that you may be receiving an important phone call and how long you think it may take. My relative did neither. She spent thirty minutes yapping, but couldn't take two minutes to give me any kind of signal that I was "allowed" to do anything other than sit on the couch, listening to her conversation.

If you can be proud of such behavior, go on with your bad self. If it were me on the phone, I would at least let my guest know that I would be with them as soon as possible. A little communication and sincerity go a long way toward righting rudeness.

Dull Razors

Let's face it—if you can remember to put gas in your car, then you should have no problem remembering to change your razor blade.

Most guys have made the mistake of shaving with a dull razor; don't let it happen to you. The pain and abrasion might not seem too bad at first, but as the blood starts to flow, you'll quickly realize what a mistake it was.

A smooth face or trimmed beard is very important, especially if you come into contact with numerous people on a daily basis. Showing up to the board meeting with your face and neck covered with Band-Aids will certainly not allow you to make your best impression.

What if it's not a board meeting but a first date? Don't spoil the evening for yourself just because of one bad blade. If you happen to do a hack job on yourself, many fine products are available to help soothe the skin and settle any redness due to irritation. Aftershave lotion is a good start, but be careful of overly scented products, which can abrade your skin further...and stink up the room!

On the subject of cologne and first dates, put a little time and effort into your wardrobe, deodorant, cologne and breath freshener, and you'll be ready to make an impression that counts. Even in the boardroom, you're bound to make a greater impact if you present yourself like a well-put-together gentleman.

No matter how poor you are, you must remember the small necessities of everyday life, and that includes a fresh razor blade. Do you want to walk around looking like one of Freddy Kruger's latest victims? I didn't think so.

Easy On the Email

Living legend Tiger Woods once made a comment on camera about the million reasons why he would rather win the American Express golf tournament than the Ryder Cup, which was being played the following week: The AMEX tournament offered a million-dollar winner's purse, so it was obvious that Tiger was trying to be humorous.

Unfortunately, many didn't get his joke, and poor Tiger's publicity people had to deal with a lot of flack for his off-the-cuff remark.

If someone can be that misunderstood on national television, imagine what could happen with email, which does not allow vocal tones or facial expressions that might help your audience better understand your remarks. This is why it's crucial to keep your emails brief and as non-confrontational as possible. The last thing you want to do is insult someone when you're trying to humor them.

Before you hit the "Send" button, make sure you've gone over everything twice. If there's any doubt of how the recipient might take anything you say, pick up the phone and speak to the person one on one, or re-edit your email until there can be no misunderstanding. You can also include your phone number, which will encourage the recipient to call you if he has any questions or concerns.

Many of us rely on email as a primary means of communication, forgetting that human beings actually read the messages we send. Protect yourself from hurting someone else's feelings by keeping your email messages short and sweet.

Enlarge This

Today, cosmetic surgery is almost as common as brushing your teeth. The only difference is that toothpaste is a little less expensive.

If someone is badly burned and needs cosmetic surgery, I'm all for it, but how many times does a woman have to keep changing the size of her chest? I was walking through the airport in Dallas, Texas, and saw a woman who must have just gone in for the "buffet" of cosmetic surgery. Her lips were so large and her face so tight that she honestly looked like Ronald McDonald. I don't like to make fun of anyone, but what I saw was not attractive.

Men these days are undergoing the knife as much as women: the nose, the eyes, basically anything to keep them looking young. I'm actually growing old trying to keep up with sixty-year-old men who look better than I do. It's costly and sometimes very effective, but on the other hand, it can be dangerous. Any time you go under the knife, something can go wrong, potentially making things worse than before you went in.

Take, for example, a basic cosmetic surgery that eliminates excess fat and wrinkles. My friend's father can no longer go swimming because of the complications from this surgery. He needs to put drops in his eyes three times a day and is also now sensitive to bright light. Tell me, is that worth the risk of losing a few wrinkles?

Before you decide to undergo elective cosmetic surgery, take a good look at yourself. You have plenty of options besides surgery for improving upon the great looks you already have.

Bobby contemplates telling Susan whether
he's excited or his pants are too big.

Erect By Default

It's a guy's worse nightmare: You're sitting in class, watching the sexiest female professor give her take on impressionistic art, and she asks you to come forward and talk about your most recent trip to a popular museum.

You feel confident, but as you try to rise out of your chair, you quickly realize there's something "down there" that's already risen. It's not a life-or-death situation, but it will be tough for your audience to keep a straight face—let alone concentrate on your discussion—as they try to keep their eyes off your "Leaning Tower of Pisa."

Odd poppings-up may be more likely to occur while you're on a date. If that's the case, try to adjust yourself so you're not so obvious. A date is more likely to understand than a class filled with students; if you're on a date and in the middle of a serious make-out session, such things are expected. It's certainly nothing to be ashamed of, but don't start trying to "Free Willy" unless your date is also thinking along those lines.

In situations like these, I return to a lasting image, one that scared the hell out of me when I was a child. My friend invited me to sleep over at his grandmother's house, and when I went to use the bathroom that night, I saw her teeth in a jar. I was a little kid, so my first thought was that she was some sort of monster. As the years went by, I realized that she was no monster, but the answer to my prayers. Whenever I find myself victim to an embarrassing and unwanted erection, I just picture her teeth. Works like a charm.

Uncontrollable erections are awkward—yet common—for most guys, so find at least one undesirable visual memory that you can pull up at any given time. I don't mean to be disrespectful my friend's grandmother, but you have to go with whatever works for you.

Fair Notice

I woke up one morning feeling like something just wasn't right. I had a sharp pain in my lower stomach and decided to drive myself to the doctor. He took a blood test and told me to go to the hospital. They offered to call an ambulance, but I decided to drive myself.

By that point, I looked like and felt like hell; the lady in the Emergency Unit must have noticed because she admitted me almost immediately. A few hours later, a nurse was about to wheel me into surgery to remove my appendix, when she asked if I had notified anyone in my family. I told her I hadn't, and she said I wasn't going one step further until I did.

If you don't have a good relationship with your family, tell a friend or a neighbor of your whereabouts so at least someone knows where you are. Plenty of people go missing each year. We don't want you to become another statistic.

My family had already spent enough time in hospitals, and I didn't want to bother them. Unfortunately, families don't work that way. To them, it doesn't matter if you're going to the hospital or on vacation; they expect communication in case something happens and they need to reach you.

I should have notified a family member on the way to the hospital. I should have given them fair notice. I was fortunate enough to have been able to drive myself to the hospital. In the case of an emergency appendectomy, many people don't have that luxury.

I've always felt you can count on family far more than you can count on anyone else, so do the right thing and keep your loved ones aware of your illnesses. It's important to them, so it should be equally important to you.

"If this is his office, what does he have
hanging at home?"

Family Portrait

My wife gives me a hard time because I don't have a picture of her on my desk at work. I explained that I see her almost every day, and it's not like I'm going to forget what she looks like. She did not appreciate my thoughts on the subject.

For women, having a picture of your significant other on your desk seems to be a security issue. They know there are other "hot" women in the office, and if you have a photograph on your desk, it's almost like posting a "Beware of Dog" sign outside your home. I'm not saying your girlfriend is a dog, but women, like dogs, seem to feel the instinctive need to protect their men.

On the other hand, I work with men who plaster their offices with photographs of their families, usually married guys with children, a wife and a few pets. You never see a single guy decorating his office with photos of his various girlfriends. Wonder why?

Personally, I think the office is a professional place, and you should limit your display of family photographs, especially if you're working at a company you don't own. Clients may come into your office and may not want to be inundated with your family album.

If you happen to work at a business you own, then please, decorate as you like. If you keep your loved ones close to your heart, why not keep them on the next closest thing, your desk? The office can be a stressful place, so an occasional smile from your wife and children may be all you need to get you through the day.

Finger Dipping

Yes, I've explored different areas of table manners ad infinitum, but some topics bear repeated discussion. The issue of finger dipping, as you may have guessed, is one such topic.

My regular office lunch gang and I decided to try to a new Tex-Mex/Southwest restaurant. The boys and I ordered fajitas, and to stave off our hunger, the waitress brought over a bowl of salsa so large that it looked like a meal in itself.

My buddy, "Finger-Dipping Frank," decided to sample the salsa before any of us had a chance to lift a chip. Unfortunately, as you've probably guessed, Frank went in fingers first, making that bowl of salsa exclusive to Frank.

He didn't think he was doing anything wrong until he looked up and saw complete disgust on each of our faces. Our response—and the threat of us breaking his fingers—enabled Frank to get the message loud and clear.

Using your finger to sample any food that is going to be shared by more than one person is a definite no-no. It doesn't matter if it's salsa or a salad bar, barbecue or a birthday cake—keep your hands off! Trust me: no one wants to share his meal with the various germs that live on your hands.

You may think you have the cleanest, most beautiful hands in the world, but they would look even better holding a pair of utensils you could use to choose whatever dish you wanted. I know it's tempting to let your fingers do the walking, but don't let them veer too far off the road of good manners.

Finish What You Start

How many projects do you start and never finish? Around the house, you may have a half-finished book lying around or a half-built deck in the backyard.

Projects, while begun with the best of intentions, can be difficult to finish, what with all the interruptions that occur in everyday life. A month can go by, and you wind up losing track of everything you started.

Your wife may rant and rave about those little house projects that you have not completed, but her wrath will hardly compare to what you will face if you fall into that pattern at work.

At my old company, a guy named Doug was gathering information on a competitor we were looking to buy out. Doug went on vacation for two weeks, even though the project was due, thinking he could finish his study upon his return. It just so happened the CEO needed that information while Doug was cocktailing in Acapulco. Doug's vacation became permanent because he didn't finish what he'd started.

Don't let this happen to you. See every task through, from beginning to end, regardless of the size. If you begin a project that you cannot complete because of various circumstances, leave yourself enough reminders to make sure you follow up as soon as possible. If you leave on vacation, inform an associate of any documents that may be needed while you're gone.

Look at every scenario before you leave, ensuring you've covered your bases. It's the little projects you complete in life that will lead to the greatest rewards.

Fly on Food

When we go out to eat, we usually order off the menu, trusting that the kitchen is clean and the food preparation flawless. However, in some cases, you can actually see the food you are about to purchase. If there's a fly hovering above that tray of freshly baked brownies, it's decision time.

I avoid those exposed food items as though they are laced with arsenic. What's the point? Unless you don't care how many flies use the French Roll as their landing strip, only eat food that is protected by plastic. Otherwise, go ahead and enjoy the baguette!

Keep your eyes open for any place food is served, including the chilled deli counter inside a supermarket. You would think the cold climate would distract any flying insects from coming close to the potato salad…think again. Those pesky flies are everywhere—as you might want to point out to the person behind the counter!

Regardless of the food item, if it's wrapped or even properly covered, then it's good enough for me. It shows that the store is thinking along the same lines as I am, and it's that common courtesy that will make me a satisfied customer.

Flies are a nuisance wherever you go. If they bother you during a meal, do your best to swat them away. If a particular restaurant appears to have more flies than paying customers, ask for a table inside or find a different restaurant. You're not going to avoid flies altogether, but you can easily find a place that does its part to keep them out.

Folding vs. Stuffing

I was never a good folder. In fact, in my mind, there wasn't much of a difference between folding my clothes and neatly stuffing everything into the bureau drawers. Same end result, right? Wrong.

I wanted to learn, but it wasn't like I could open up the *Yellow Pages* and look up "Professional Folding Seminars." Finally, I took matters into my own hands and started making use of sales associates whenever I went shopping for clothes. I must admit, it was a little embarrassing having complete strangers show me how to fold a shirt properly, but the advice was free, and I put it to good use.

If you are curious as to what you should fold, you may be surprised to find that everything, including socks, shirts and underwear, are part of the package. Start with the socks...take two socks and line them up, toe-to-toe and heel-to-heel. Fold them in half. While holding the neck at one end, push the toes of both socks through. This technique will save the elastic and enable you to have one impressive sock drawer. See, wasn't that easy?

Learning to fold your socks properly may not seem like much of a critical life skill, but it will impress the ladies...or anyone else who might be rummaging through your sock or underwear drawer.

If you have a girlfriend, perhaps she can lend a helping hand. I believe that's one of the reasons men get married, so they never have to fold. If you're unmarried, you can always go back and learn from the one person who folded everything for you—your mother.

Bob spends so much time in the bathroom
that the mailman delivers all the reading
material straight to the door.

Freshen Up

If a person is capable of using a bathroom, shouldn't they have the common courtesy to spray a little air freshener when they're done?

My old roommate didn't believe she could stink up a bathroom. She said that she was a woman and women always smell sweet. I told her that while she was one of the sweetest-smelling women on whom I've ever laid nostrils, whatever she was doing in the bathroom was in complete violation of the "Sweetness Act."

I tried to break it to her gently, but it was important that she understand that when she used the bathroom for…ahem…larger jobs, it smelled like she was like giving birth to Godzilla. In order to avoid prosecution, she would have to pick up a can of Wizard and give it a few pumps.

Wanda was her name, and even though she sprayed a few times during her two-year stint as my roommate, it was usually me who took action. I would simply stick the tip of the air freshener into the gap between the floor and the door, and then give it one quick pump so Wanda wouldn't suffocate. Actually, I'm surprised she didn't suffocate when she *wasn't* using it.

I didn't mind, though. In fact, I became familiar with all the popular Wizard scents. My favorites are Mountain Berry, Botanical Garden and Country Peach.

I may not be able to afford a Mercedes Benz, but I can certainly splurge when it comes time to leaving the bathroom smelling fresh. If you have any doubt about how you leave a bathroom, do yourself a favor and put your faith in air freshener.

Getting Ahead in Bed

Have you ever slept with someone for the sake of bettering your career? It would be simple for me to tell you not to do it, but we all know how the mind and body work when clothes come off...

I can only offer advice based on the experiences of individuals I know, men who have completed the deal. In a word or seven, things didn't work out to their benefit. Only one guy did not let the woman get the best of him; for the most part, the woman takes over as the controlling party. She's the one who ended up wearing the boxer shorts, and more often than not, they were his.

Let's take a look at what's really at stake: pride, self-esteem, freedom and individuality. Once you have slept with someone at work, there's no going back and no retrieving your lost values... or lost reputation.

You may think you are in love with the top female vice-president. However, chances are it's a crush—not the real deal at all—or maybe just not yet. Perhaps you fancy a new co-worker or your sexy boss. The bottom line is that you are taking a huge risk. The results may work for or against you. If you leave the relationship at merely a friendship and don't bring sex into the equation, you have a much greater chance of keeping your job intact.

There is always the possibility that the two of you really are in love and will end up sharing a beautiful life together. You take over the company, while she stays home and takes care of the children. Stranger things have happened, so before you cross the line, ask your heart if the two of you have genuine feelings for one another, and the decision should be simple.

Girl, Interrupted

I was watching a popular talk show the other day and noticed that the four female hostesses could not stop walking over one another's lines. I thought, "For crying out loud, ladies, let someone finish a thought!"

Being interrupted is sometimes more annoying than sitting in traffic. People are so eager to make a point that they simply forget someone else is talking. Hence, there's a true art to listening and allowing people to finish their thoughts.

A well-known Hollywood story tells of a successful screenwriting team that broke up because of rude interruptions. Whenever this man-and-woman team took a pitch meeting, the man would start talking before the woman had a chance to finish her sentences. She finally got tired of his lack of respect toward her and dissolved the partnership.

It's easy to get the creative juices flowing and throw out new ideas as soon as they pop up, but it doesn't give anyone the right to interrupt other ideas being presented. Wait for the right moment to speak, as opposed to blurting out the first thought that comes to mind.

Interrupting a meeting is a different story. Perhaps your boss is in a meeting but he's waiting for an important phone call. When that call comes in and you have to poke your head into the boardroom, don't forget to say "excuse me" before you say anything else. Be polite, but also explain the urgency of this interruption.

No matter what the situation is, if you're going to interrupt, be quick about it and to the point. However, avoid interrupting if you can, especially when someone else is talking. You may earn more respect by learning to listen than always trying to get in your two-cents.

Give and Take

I'm not big on receiving gifts, a bad habit of which I'm not too proud. Hardheaded fools like me don't understand—or can't accept—that people enjoy giving as much as they like to receive.

People give gifts because it makes them feel good. I, on the other hand, don't like to see friends or family spend their money on something I'm not going to use. Proper etiquette tells us that their finances are none of my business and that I should not stand in the way of whatever might make them happy.

Whatever you do, don't make the same stupid mistakes I made in the past. One year for my birthday, I went out and bought a gift for myself. It was actually supposed to be from my family, but I thought if I gave them the receipt, they would be happy to know I got something I wanted.

Little did I know that my family was more interested in the element of surprise rather than letting me do the shopping for them. I still think it's better to receive gifts you actually want and can use, but even I have to accept that sometimes we all receive horrible, useless gifts a family member or close friend had selected with love.

Nowadays, my family and I meet in the middle: I present them with a wish list of several items I'd like or would find useful. The odds are in my favor that I'll end up with something I like.

You can also do things the traditional way and not say anything at all, hoping for the best. Regardless of the gift, be sure to show appreciation to those who spend their time and money shopping for you. It's the proper thing to do.

Hard-Headed Fool

Men sometimes let their stubbornness get in the way of making great advances in life. Take, for example, the way a man treats a woman.

Men become so caught up in their own little worlds that they tend to forget about women and their needs. Women want to spend time with their boyfriends, but sometimes the boyfriend wants to spend time with his buddies instead. A woman will only put up with that kind of behavior for so long before she moves on to another man who will give her the attention she needs. When that time comes, the boyfriend will hit himself for being so stubborn, and she will be one more special woman who got away.

I may have used "boyfriends" as an example in the above paragraph, but if you're a husband, don't think I'm letting you off the hook. Why is the divorce rate in California above fifty percent? It's not because married men are spending so much quality time with their wives, that's for sure. Whether you're married or not, make enough time for the woman who loves you the most.

Here's another example of men and their stubbornness: My brother was looking to buy a house. He finally found one, but when it came time to buy, he was outbid. He was so stubborn that he refused to submit another bid. After losing another dream house, he was reluctant to look at any more homes, thinking there was nothing out there for him. For the next two years, he threw away money, renting a place when he could have turned that money into equity.

You have to be ready to take chances, whether it's with a woman or a piece of real estate. Put your stubbornness aside and just go for it—you don't know how wonderful your life can be until you take a risk.

Hats Off

On one episode of the popular TV show, *The Sopranos*, Tony was trying to enjoy himself inside a fancy restaurant, but became distracted by some punk wearing a baseball cap. Tony sent one of his thugs over to tell the kid to remove the hat from his head or have his head removed from his body.

I'm only the author of this book—I am not trying to make you an offer you can't refuse, but I'm here to tell you that no matter what public place you're in, the hat comes off.

Women are the exception; they can wear hats almost anywhere they want. If a woman chooses to keep her hat on, it should flow with the rest of her outfit, not stick out like a sore thumb. In Los Angeles, it's trendy for women to wear baseball caps and pull their hair through the cap, much like a ponytail. In this situation, the cap is more than a hat; it's part of the ensemble. However, for formal affairs or in ritzy restaurants, baseball caps should always be removed, regardless of whether you're a man or woman.

Once, when I was in a movie theater, I had to ask the gentleman in front of me to remove his cap. It's a little hard to believe that I even had to ask, but if that should ever happen to you, be polite and not rude. If he is considerate and removes his cap, great, but if he raises a stink, here's what you can do: move your seat, alert an employee or call Tony Soprano.

Haven't Heard From You

If you call someone, you shouldn't have to wait more than a week to hear back from that person. The only exceptions are death, hospitalization or laryngitis.

I've been buried at work, to the point where it feels like I'm barely hanging on, and yet I've managed to return phone calls. It's unfortunate when you're that busy, because everything else in your life is put on hold, including friends. The problem is that your friends have no idea you're busy, so they can very easily think you're blowing them off.

If you don't have time to talk, leave a voicemail—or send an email. You can certainly do something to let your callers know you're alive and well. If you want to avoid becoming caught in potentially endless conversations, think beforehand and call when the person is unlikely to be home. Leave a message that explains your deadlines, and promise to call back for a real conversation when you're caught up at work.

Family should always be a priority when it comes time to returning calls. Nine times out of ten, your sister will call to bug you about something stupid, but there's always that possibility that something is seriously wrong. My sister usually calls to complain that I don't call my father enough, and then when I call my father, he tells me he wishes my sister would stop calling so much.

Your friends and family will always be glad to hear from you, no matter how little personal time you have to spare. It's better to call for five minutes than not to call at all.

Having a Ball in the Hall

It's three a.m., and you and your loved one are enjoying a deep sleep after a memorable night in Las Vegas. Earlier that evening, you had a wonderful dinner and saw a spectacular show. What you didn't plan for was being woken up by loud and obnoxious individuals heading back to their room in the wee hours of the night.

It boggles my mind—it's almost as elementary as two plus two—but hotel hallway noise is simple fact. It doesn't matter if you're in Las Vegas or Rio de Janeiro: People walking through the hallway of a hotel can simply forget that other people nearby are trying to sleep.

Common courtesy dictates that when the sun goes down, people go to sleep. Sure, not everyone hits the hay at sunset. Some people stay up until two in the morning; others stay up all night. However, many people, young and old, retire a few hours after sundown, and hotel guests should respect their right to do so.

Of course, those who have been drinking or doing drugs have a greater tendency to believe that there is no one else on the planet but them. However, if you're not under the influence of anything except "stupid pills," there's no excuse for obnoxious behavior. Try not talk until you get into your room.

Once you are inside your room, please remember the time. The volume of your voice and the television should be kept down. If the front desk calls to warn you about the noise coming from your room, that's *not* the time to turn up the music. Chances are you're not a rock star, and if the front desk calls, you should probably stop partying like one.

Hank may be handicapped, but his psychic
powers come in handy at the market.

Help the Handicapped

I was occupied with my normal three-hour tour inside Home Depot, when I passed by a woman wearing an orthopedic brace around her wrist. Ironically, she was about to pick up a twenty-pound cinderblock. I offered to help and she gladly accepted, saying that I must have experienced a similar injury to be so insightful. I just nodded and told her that I like to help out when I can.

One may not consider someone wearing an orthopedic wrist brace to be "handicapped," but I do. It's not the same as being in a wheelchair, but this woman had an injury that would have probably caused her pain if she had attempted to lift the concrete block on her own. She paid me a wonderful compliment following my good deed, but I didn't do it for brownie points. I did it because it was the right thing to do.

Be aware of those around you and what you might do to make their lives a little easier. It might be something as simple as pulling two stuck shopping carts apart for an elderly person if he can't seem to do it on his own. Perhaps someone in a wheelchair needs help grabbing an item off a shelf? Grab it for her. See a pregnant woman trying to load heavy bags in her car? Why not ask if you can help? The answer might be "no," but at least you offered.

The list of ways you can help others is endless, as should be your willingness to help. Remember not to force yourself on the person if he or she says "No, thank you," but don't be afraid to make the offer. Like I said, it's the right thing to do.

Who says a guy can't be productive
when his wife is out of town?

Helping Hand

It's truly wonderful to be congratulated for performing proper etiquette in a public place. It's not so wonderful when the person who acknowledged you for your good deed does not turn around and do the same for someone else.

I was at the local supermarket, going through the checkout line, when I grabbed a divider and put it down so the woman behind me could put her groceries on the conveyer belt as well. She politely tapped me on the shoulder, and as I turned around, she lit up the market with her smile, greeting me with a warm "thank you." Without hesitation, I returned an even warmer "you're welcome," and between the two of us, we melted a bag of ice that was in the shopping cart behind her. However, her next move surprised me: Ms. Heatmeizer thanked me for putting a divider down for her, but she didn't do it for Mr. Ice Man, who was behind her!

Funny how that works; it's like holding the door open for one person, but not the other, or allowing one car to merge, but not two. As you can tell, I have given this much thought, and still can't come up with a reasonable explanation for her behavior— unless my overwhelming charm took her by surprise, erasing her memory of what to do next.

If you are ever a recipient of someone doing a good deed for you, don't wait a year to return the favor. Acknowledge the gesture, and be aware of how you can do the same for someone else. The world turns around for a reason, and if you haven't figured it out, it's because of good people like you!

"What kind of insurance doesn't consider
ELK a road hazard?!?"

Hit and Never Run

If you hit someone with your car and take off without leaving any sort of information, you have committed a crime. You may think you're getting away with it, but, in the game of life, your actions will certainly catch up to you.

Let's say the damage comes to $300. Take that $300 and weigh it against your peace of mind for the rest of your life. Is it worth living with that on your guilty conscious that long, for a measly $300? I didn't think so.

The same holds true if you witness an accident or someone inflicting damage to another automobile. While the ultimate sacrifice would be to leave your name and phone number, people these days just don't want to get involved. However, just because you don't want to leave your name doesn't mean you can't leave some information about the person who did the damage, possibly the license plate number and the make and model of the offending car.

Most neighborhoods now have community-watch programs, in which residents take responsibility for looking after one another's homes, not just their own. I started a little program just with the houses surrounding mine. My neighbors and I exchanged phone numbers, including a number where we can be reached if we're away from home in case of an emergency. Something so simple has already proven to go a long way.

This isn't brain surgery; it's just doing what you're supposed to do. After all, etiquette has everything to do with being an honest and respectable human being.

Preparation can kill a guy.

Home Alone

One of the greatest benefits of living with a woman is that she doesn't allow you to sit on your butt. Nevertheless, the greatest time for a man who has moved in with a woman is the precious moments when she's out of the house. Don't get me wrong: Nothing can detract from the joy of being together, but everyone needs his down time.

What you do with your down time is always a concern. Let's take a look at a few favorite options: eat, sleep, watch television or enjoy other forms of adult entertainment. Now, let's take a look at a few other, less popular options: cook, clean, shop or finish all the chores you promised would be done a month ago.

I think the best solution is to compromise. Mow the lawn, and then watch the game. During half time, get up and take care of the laundry. When the game ends, defrost a couple of steaks to grill for dinner.

Which would you rather have, a woman who comes home and yells at you for doing nothing all day or one who comes home, takes note of your good works, and then escorts you to the bedroom for a different kind of down time?

Rise to the occasion, gentlemen, and bring the multitasking abilities you developed at work into to your home. You can have your down time, but help out where you can so that she can have a little down time, too. The rewards will be innumerable.

How to Respond

There's nothing more frustrating than holding a door open for someone and not being acknowledged, especially when you have to wait for him to reach the door. A "thank you" would be nice, even appropriate, but I'll settle for a smile, if that's all you have to offer.

I'm happy to confirm that there are more people who say "thank you" than not. What makes me such an expert? I don't care if you're black, white, fat, thin, male or female—I'll hold the door open for you, regardless.

It doesn't require a college education to figure out that people enjoy having the door held for them, just the ability to perform proper etiquette. While I never tire of hearing someone say "Thank you," if I don't hear it, I still respond with "You're welcome," without being rude. Sometimes that simple phrase is enough for the person to realize he's made a mistake. Sometimes, the person will even be grateful you pointed out his "forgetfulness."

Of course there are those who think they are better than the rest of us, and will not respond even if you try to make conversation. In that case, I will not hold the door open for you because your head is too big to get through it.

Another popular action that seldom receives a response is saying, "How are you?" People may think you're just saying hello, as opposed to actually wanting to know how they are doing. You can interpret the greeting however you want, but if the person acknowledged you, try to return the gesture. You don't have to get into a drawn-out explanation of what's going on in your life; a simple "fine, thank you" will do.

Whether you give a warm "thank you" or a simple "hello," discover how nice your life can be when you communicate with others. It's quick and simple, and it's good etiquette.

I'm Not Famous

Life is difficult. It certainly doesn't help when a bunch of close friends have become successful, and you're still struggling to pay rent. Monetary status affects almost everything you do—who wants to be the token "loser" in the group?

Allow me to clarify: Just because you don't make a lot of money, it doesn't make you a loser. It certainly makes you uncomfortable, however, especially where money issues comes into play. Unfortunately, unless your friends are into getting together at the library to read, money is usually an issue. Don't try to compete with the big boys if you don't measure up in the wallet.

What do you do? You can find a new circle of friends, see the successful pals only when you can afford it or find some way to deal with the situation. Life is too short to have feelings of self-pity, so do everything you can to keep your friends as you live within your means.

If your rich pals want to pick up the tab for the steak dinner, beautiful. Just don't make a habit of it. If they want to invite you to their country club to play a round of golf, go for it, but don't call them and invite yourself.

There are things you can do to extend yourself that won't cost an arm and a leg. Invite them over to watch a football game. Your total investment will be the potato chips and a few six packs of beer. At least you're making an effort!

Let's not forget that there are three classes here in America; if it weren't for the middle class, there would be no upper or lower. The most important thing to remember is that a good friendship should have nothing to do with money, but everything to do with kindness and trust.

In and Out of Love

Well, it's over. After seeing one girl for the last two years, you've decided to move on. A part of you wants to take your phone off the hook and not deal with anyone for a while, but your friends want you to get back out there and pick up where you left off.

I may not have all the answers, but I can share a few basic pointers for soothing your soul. I use the word "soul" because that's where the pain is coming from, and until you give your soul a little down time, you're not really going to have a fun time.

You should grow a little more with every relationship. In order to do so, you may want to read a little on the subject. Self-help books really key in on many of the unanswered questions left over from your breakup; reading about how to find the answers will better prepare you for when you're ready to get serious with someone else. Dozens of wonderful self-help books are out there; I'm sure you can find one that is suitable for you.

If you are stubborn, like me, you might not think you need help. However, think of it as an education—reading about relationships is like taking a class in school. The more you study, the better you'll do on the final.

If reading isn't your cup of tea, try an intimate night of conversation with a close friend, maybe even a married couple, who can help with your pain or confusion and allow you to get things off your chest. Many people turn to therapists, feeling more secure with a professional opinion. If you spend a lot of time in the car, look into getting a self-help audio book.

Regardless of which way you turn, do something for yourself; don't bottle in the pain. If you do, you will bring that baggage into your next relationship, and that isn't fair to either you or her.

In Style

Clothes play such an important role in today's society; they not only make the man, but label him, too.

The clothes you wear help form opinions—that's how Mr. Blackwell is able to make a living. Do you think anyone wants to be on his worst-dressed list? Probably not, but what you wear doesn't just open the door to criticism; it offers you a way to garner compliments, too.

Try to dress appropriately for the situation. I knew a guy in college who wore suits to class, while everyone else wore baggy shorts and T-shirts. To this day, I can't recall any of his athletic or academic achievements. What do I remember is that his clothes were not appropriate for a college campus—at least the one I attended.

If you work in a big office, find a happy medium with your wardrobe choice. Try to fit in and not stick out. If you work in the mailroom, leave the three-piece suit at home. You don't want to wear a nicer suit than the one your boss wears. You're there to do a job, not put on a fashion show.

You don't need expensive clothes to look good, just a little fashion expertise. Make yourself presentable, and don't show up looking like a slob. Tuck in your shirt, and wear a belt. Avoid tennis shoes, and polish those wing tips at least once a month. Shop around for bargains, and try to put together an outfit rather than a shirt here and a pair of pants there.

A strong outfit will raise you from a normal guy to a super stud, so be proud of your body and the clothes you put on it.

Invite Yourself

It's always an awkward and unusual moment when you are expecting an invitation, but don't receive one.

I was at a friend's 40th birthday party, which took place at his house, the dream house about which I can only dream—everything about the place is breathtaking, including his art collection.

When I arrived at the party (to which I *was* invited), I said hello to "Birthday Boy Bill," who informed me that he was about to give another invitee the official "tour de house." The next thing I expected to hear was, "Why don't you come along," but all I got was silence.

In that situation, many people would have simply invited themselves along. However, I feel that if the invitation is not extended to you, then there may be a reason why your no-longer-potential host wants to be alone, a reason you should respect until notified otherwise.

In a separate incident, my wife and I took a trip to one of our favorite destinations, Canada. We have friends who live there, and sometimes they even call to find out when we are planning our next visit. We received such a call from "The Swanson's," and upon crossing the border, we called them to let them know we had arrived.

Although they were excited to hear from us, not once did they suggest we get together. *How odd,* I thought, but my wife and I both agreed that we should not push the issue. If they wanted to get together, they would certainly suggest it. We left our number where we could be reached, but never heard from them. Life goes on, and we still consider them friends.

Never force yourself on someone else if you don't receive an invitation. You'll only pressure your hosts into extending one, regardless of their wishes, which creates an uncomfortable situation for all.

Just Shy of Stalking

Breaking up sometimes feels like a living hell, but it doesn't compare with the real hell you put your ex through when you refuse to let go. Women can freak out as much as men do; regardless of the gender, it's the same pain.

I knew a guy who couldn't wait to break up with his girlfriend, but once he did, he literally went crazy without her. He would call twenty times an hour, show up unexpectedly at her work and follow her as she drove around town. If you fall into this category, do yourself a favor and get help. It's not fair to you or your former lover.

More trouble erupts when the pseudo-stalker feels he doesn't need help. As a friend, do everything in your power to make sure he's okay. It may mean picking up the phone and calling his relatives or driving him somewhere he won't be alone. His world has been shattered, but with a friend nearby, it's easier to pick up the pieces.

If it's you who's doing the damage and scaring your ex on a daily basis, then you're wasting your time. Think about it. You're desperately trying to get back with someone you probably tried to get away from. It's time to come to your senses and realize she's not the one for you.

Go to the movies. Go out with friends. Go check out an online dating service. Whatever you do, stop causing fear in other people's lives. They don't deserve it, and you're not doing anything to help yourself.

Keep Calm During Construction

Don't you hate it when your neighbors begin construction on their house? Yes, it will look nice when it's done, and yes, the neighborhood will probably be a better place because of it, but you know you'll have to deal with nonstop noise for the next few months.

No matter where you live, if you're going to start construction that may cause excessive noise, let your neighbors know, so you don't take them by surprise. If you don't get along with a particular neighbor, leave a note on his door. If the construction falls behind schedule—although I've *never* heard of that happening!—keep your neighbors posted so they don't wonder when the noise will stop.

How do you distinguish excessive noise? If the twenty million barking dogs in your neighborhood become a pleasant diversion from the racket in your backyard, then you're creating excessive noise.

If you're close with a particular neighbor, don't leave them out of the loop. Perhaps you want to invite them over during the course of construction so they can witness your home's transformation. I've known neighbors who actually pointed out flaws that the grateful homeowner didn't catch.

Once the project is complete, you may want to bring your neighbors a little gift for being patient: a bottle of wine, a plate of cookies, a citronella candle for their now-quiet backyards. However, why not invite them over to see the new addition? At the same time, have a barbecue and make a night of it. A friend of mine built a pool, and then had a block party, so nobody felt slighted.

If you're going to create noise in the neighborhood, fulfill your responsibility of keeping peace in the neighborhood, as well.

In order to stay close to the buffet,
Iris became part of the buffet.

Keeping Food a Secret

I recently attended a wine-tasting event at which they poured a variety of wines and served a wide assortment of appetizers. Despite the culinary display, I couldn't take my eyes off one woman, who engulfed each appetizer as a whole, as opposed to taking small bites. She looked as if her cheek was swollen because there was always something in it.

Whether you're at a cocktail party or a sit-down dinner, take small bites. A mouth stuffed full of food is not flattering for anyone, male or female. You also want to avoid turning the party into a war-zone with your mouth shooting out shrapnel at innocent passer-bys.

Once food reaches the mouth, it should remain a secret. The fact that you're chewing with your mouth closed—I hope!—is evidence enough that you are feeding yourself. Don't all of a sudden become a squirrel and start packing it in for the winter to come.

At buffets, people simply go out of their minds when it comes to eating. They seem to feel that if they don't stack their plates sky high, and then eat as quickly as possible, they may never see food again. The truth is that they *won't* see food again...their huge bellies will get in the way.

I've witnessed this behavior on sea cruises and figured it is the main reason the different lines have to build bigger ships—not to hold more people, but to hold the same people who are growing larger from buffet over-consumption.

Everyone needs to slow down and enjoy the eating process. Taking time with your meal will make each dining experience more enjoyable, and probably add a few years to your life.

Know When to Pour

Whether you're having a sit-down dinner or a casual barbecue, you can count on one thing whenever you entertain: plenty of drinks.

Considerate guests bring flowers, a dessert, possibly a bottle of wine. However, unless you've made prior arrangements with your dinner guests, assume that it will be you providing the hooch and stock up.

Regardless of what you're serving for dinner, chances are good that you'll be opening at least one bottle of wine. Because both red and white wine will be in demand, make sure you have at least one of each, with the appropriate glassware, whenever possible.

As the host, it is your responsibility to make sure your guests' glasses are filled at all times. That doesn't mean that every time someone takes a sip you need to hurry to their sides to top off their wine glass. At the same time, they should never be waiting too long if their glass is empty. The same holds true for any beverage, alcoholic or not.

The only exception is when you're dealing with a drunkard. If you've been making sure your cousin, Gus, has a cold one in front of him, and Gus is starting to slur his speech, switch the Coors to a Coke, and tell Gus he's had enough. If Gus starts to get belligerent, remind him that he's not at one of his weekend pubs, but at a family affair. If Gus still doesn't respond, pull out an old photo album to prove that he's actually a part of the family.

As the host, you can also be held liable if any of your guests gets into an accident after they leave. Keep this in mind when you pour, and, more importantly, know when to hold.

Lap-Dance Fever

One of the greatest pleasures a man can experience at least once in his life is a lap-dance. Whether you are at a strip club, gentleman's club or bachelor party, you should respect proper etiquette during these three minutes of pleasure.

Keep your pants on. I'm speaking on behalf of myself and the lovely lady who is charging you twenty-five dollars a dance. You might think she's coming onto you, but that's her job, and you're no more special than the fifty other guys whose laps she'll be dancing on as the night progresses.

Give yourself a budget, and stick to it. One lap dance goes by fairly quickly. When she asks if you want another, the next song has already started and so has she. By the time you leave that booth, you may be taking out a second mortgage on your home.

Know when to say goodbye. I went with two other friends to one of the local clubs. One guy hooked up with a dancer early, and when my other buddy and I wanted to leave, the first guy did not. Unfortunately, he had driven, so we were forced to take a taxi. When a lap dance becomes more important than your friends, don't be surprised if they're not your friends the following day.

Finally, remember that most dancers have children and are counting on your business to support their families. You are not special; you are rent and food on the table. While you may be thinking that she wants you stay because she likes you, she knows if you stay she'll be able to buy her son that baseball glove he so desperately wants.

Enjoy each lap dance for what it is, but remember that the "romance" is over once the music ends.

Leave Now

What can you do to get guests to leave? You don't want to be rude, but you don't want a pleasant visit to deteriorate into a situation in which your once-welcome guests become pains in the butt.

I like to drop a line at the beginning of the evening indicating that the visit will be a finite, bound by some time restriction. Then, whatever you say later, you won't seem as though you are trying to get rid of your guests.

I love to golf, so I've often told my guests that I have an early tee time the following morning. Of course, I don't hit them with that piece of news as soon as they walk in...I wait a while and drop it into normal conversation.

Golf works well because early tee times are synonymous with the sport; a seven-a.m. basketball game may be a tougher sell. Use your imagination, but find a reasonable explanation for why your guests need to leave.

When the visit reaches a point when you think there's no way they'll want you to open another bottle of wine, but they do, that's when you need to stand up, look them in the eye and say, "You know what, that's going to do it for me." It's all about putting your foot down—politely—no matter how many guests you have.

Start cleaning up, if that's what it takes. Take any bottles or dishes into the kitchen, and begin to wrap up whatever food remains. If you're in a giving mood, you can even fix a plate for them to take home, which might soften the blow of your foot on their butts as you kick them out the front door.

For those with guests who can't take a hint, I offer the following advice: Once you get them out, don't invite them back.

Line Cutter

Line cutting has to be one of the most annoying things anyone can do in public. Here's an example: You're waiting at the supermarket, and you've allowed a respectable amount of space between your shopping cart and the cart in front of you. You're killing time by browsing through one of the tabloids, and, when you look up, "Irwin the Inconsiderate" has decided to wedge his cart in front of yours.

Of course, your natural reaction might be to give him the stink-eye and say something nasty, but you are a respectable shopper and citizen of your community, so you simply make it clear that there is a line, and he should find the back of it. Irwin's normal reaction is usually, "Oh, I didn't realize there was a line"…which makes me wonder if Irwin knows what planet he's on.

Ladies and gentlemen, this happens all the time. I was in a donut shop, where a man bypassed the line and walked right up to the counter. He was there for five minutes before he figured out there was a line. I was at a crowded airport when a woman ran to the front of the security line, pleading with others to let her in because she was late for a flight. We let her in, she didn't say thank you and you know what? She missed her flight.

You can find line cutters wherever there are lines. If you—or someone—doesn't say something, guys like Irwin will continue to do as they please. It's all about karma, ladies and gentlemen. Actually it's all about waiting in line.

When Joe's not cleaning pools, he's
cleaning up the streets.

Litterbug

A piece of chewing gum goes flying out the car window…a walk on the beach generates a soda can left in the sand…a table clears at your favorite fast-food restaurant, but the people who vacated the table left all their trash behind for the next person to clean up.

We live in a society where people are so prone to littering that it would take electroshock therapy—not a mere $1,000 fine—to get them to stop trash on the ground. I'm not a big fan of electroshock therapy or hefty fines, so let's try to find a cure within this chapter.

Litterbugs know what they're doing—they're just too lazy or too inconsiderate to do the right thing. I attack the problem the best way I know how: If I witness someone littering and have a chance to say something, I will.

I was driving one day, and a hamburger wrapper flew out the window of the car in front of me and landed on my windshield. At the next stoplight, I pulled up next to the guilty party, showed him the wrapper and said, "I'm glad you didn't Super-Size it!" He laughed, but once the laughter died down, I told him there was nothing funny about littering. I waited for an apology, but when the light turned green, he took off. At least he didn't give me the finger.

When faced with a litterbug, all you can do is hope for the best. If you get every other person to learn from his mistakes, then you've made the world twice as clean. It's all about doing what's right, and once you've done that, living with yourself becomes a whole lot easier.

Lost & Found

You just dropped off your friend at the airport when you notice a suspicious-looking duffle bag sitting alone in the parking lot. Curiosity killed the cat, but you're hoping to escape with no more than a bruise. Inside the bag is a little more than you bargained for, almost twenty-thousand dollars more! So, when all is said and done and you come back down to planet Earth, are you going to keep the money or report it to the authorities?

Hardly a day goes by when a similar scenario doesn't play out for at least ten of us, although it might be a something on a slightly smaller scale. For instance, you might witness a five-dollar bill falling out of someone's pocket. That's a no brainer—you give it back to its rightful owner.

If it's a duffel bag filled with dough, I know it's tempting, but you should report it to the police. Here's my philosophy: it's dirty money, and however long it takes you to spend it or how much fun you have doing so, it will always be dirty money. If that doesn't faze you, go ahead and buy yourself a new used Cadillac.

Let's say the found item isn't cash, but has a large cash value. Women lose their jewelry all the time, and men have been known to go through a few fine watches, too. You can always return the item to a trustworthy vendor in the area or post a sign describing what you found and where the owner can contact you.

Your phone might start ringing off the hook with some of the neighborhood's finest, but when the rightful owner calls and identifies the item, you'll know...and you'll feel the certain sense of peace and accomplishment that accompanies doing the right thing.

"I don't have any paper, so why don't
I write my number on your head?"

Make That Move Again

Back when I was single, an incident took place that made me stop and think about the timing of meeting new women. It was a day like any other day, except for an appointment I had to see my doctor, whose office was inside a large medical building with four elevators.

On my way out, I rode down with a very attractive woman. She looked at me, and I looked at her. I was about to say something, when it occurred to me that I was not in an appropriate location for meeting new women. I was in a medical building—the woman I was about to hit on may have had something traumatic happen to her!

Of course, there's always the possibility that she only had a wart removed from her finger, but my whereabouts were certainly worth considering before laying on the thick stuff. Better yet, wait until she leaves the building, so she has a little time to forget about the doctor—and whatever news she may have received.

Funerals are right up there on the top-ten list of insensitive places to pick up chicks. What could you possibly say to a woman as you watch someone being buried? "He was a good man...he'll be missed by all...but not as much as I'll miss you if I don't get your number." Wait until the reception following the funeral to make your move.

Guys are like wolves: There's not much they'll stop at when it comes to meeting women. I won't ask you to change your habits; I'm simply telling you to be aware of where you are when you hit on women.

Married At Sea

Not long ago, I received a wedding announcement informing me that close friends had been on a Mediterranean cruise and decided to get married.

"Good for them," I thought, but as the news started to spread, not everyone shared my sentiments. Another married couple was actually insulted that they had not been invited to the ceremony and another couple thought it was selfish that the newlyweds hadn't tied the knot closer to home. These once friendly couples boycotted the marriage and didn't even bother to pick up the phone to say congratulations.

Respect whatever decision the bride and groom make. It's their wedding, and it really does not involve anyone else but them. Of course, it would be nice if they had included their respective families, but once again, the decision was entirely up to them.

No matter where the wedding takes place, if you receive an invitation, proper etiquette states that you are expected to buy a gift. If you were not invited to the wedding, you have no gift responsibilities. However, if you choose to buy a wedding gift, as you are perfectly welcome to do, the newly-marrieds would probably love it. If the newlyweds are close friends, you might want to take them out for dinner to celebrate their blessed union.

If the wedding is overseas, such as in Europe or Hawaii, and bride and groom invite family and friends, including you, then you should feel honored they thought of you. Due to the financial impact, do not feel obligated to go. If you can afford to attend the wedding, I'm sure it would be a wonderful experience. Whether you decide to attend the wedding or not, never decline without offering a sincere apology.

Mr. Wilson

Every neighborhood has one crusty old man who couldn't smile if his life depended on it. If your dog takes one step onto his lawn, there will be hell to pay. If your stereo is a little too loud, he'll call the cops.

How do you handle such a neighbor? Kill him with kindness, and he won't know what hit him. Send him a Christmas card during the holiday season, and, if you happen know the date of his birthday, do a little something on that day, too. You'll go from enemy to ally quicker than he can say "formaldehyde."

Once you get on his good side, make sure you stay there by doing the unexpected good deed. Bring in his trash containers every now and then. Walk his Sunday paper up to his front doorstep. The poor guy will be beside himself! Then, when he least expects it, start to take control of his mind. I'm kidding, of course, but don't be afraid to point out the goodness in your fellow neighbors, so he doesn't continue to build up hate.

Maybe old Mr. Wilson isn't as receptive as you initially thought. To that, I say: persistence. Play his game for a while. Go head to head, and don't back down. I don't mean that you should use a harsh tone or be rude to him, but don't allow him to get the best of you. He's probably just testing you, anyway. Once you pass muster—whatever that might be—you'll probably earn his grudging respect.

However nasty the old curmudgeon gets, return his actions with acts of kindness—unless, of course, he begins poisoning neighborhood pets or the water supply. It's not asking a lot—isn't keeping peace in the neighborhood worth it?

"Now that you know my name,
it's only fair that you tell me your name,
and your phone number."

Nametags

We live in a society in which many working Americans have to wear nametags when they're on the job. As a customer, you might then wonder if it's appropriate to address these unfortunate folks by name when shopping in their stores.

For instance, imagine you're in a fast-food joint. Do you walk up to the counter and say, "Hello, Phil, may I please have Quarter Pounder with cheese?" It feels presumptuous, as though you know Phil and ordering burgers from him is a regular thing for the two of you.

What makes the situation even more peculiar is that these employees have no idea what your name might be, so they can't even reciprocate with the same familiarity.

It's really quite amusing when you walk up to the counter and call an employee by his first name. It usually takes him a second or two to realize he's wearing his name on his chest, because he gives you a look that says, "How the hell does he know my name?" Once he comes around, you can usually expect a warm reaction. Your greeting shows you have an interest in this person, regardless of his position in life.

For the record, most people don't take advantage of nametags; they avoid addressing people by their first name when they haven't been properly introduced...which is not to say that addressing a store employee by his first name is inappropriate.

If you're up to the challenge and your fast-food experience was everything and more, introduce yourself before you leave. You know Phil's name, why shouldn't he know yours? You will surely be coming back, and it's always nice to know people on the inside, especially when there are French fries involved.

No Surprises

For you single, successful guys who can afford to take a woman away for a weekend—especially if it's the first time—don't let there be any uncomfortable surprises. I'm not talking about a bottle of champagne waiting in the room when you arrive at that darling B&B; I'm talking sleeping arrangements—how many beds will be in the room?

If the two of you have been intimate prior to your weekend away, then a conversation may not be necessary. However, if it's a first-time vacation for the two of you, then it may help to be on the same page. You might want sex, and she might just want to cuddle. Perhaps she only wants a physical relationship, and you want something more. There's any number of possibilities.

A buddy of mine from New York met a girl in Los Angeles when he came to visit me. One month later, they decided to meet in Las Vegas, because neither had ever been to Sin City. Prior to the trip, they flirted extensively via email. When I asked him if he had spelled out what he was expecting, he said, "No."

To this day, he thanks me for insisting that they talk prior to the trip because it made her feel comfortable, and she respected him even more. As things turned out, they never left their hotel room, but their tryst may not have been possible if the lines of communication hadn't been opened.

Live by this rule: always tell her where you're coming from so there are no awkward surprises. I'm not talking about email; I'm talking about picking up the phone, or better yet, telling her in person. You will win her over, for sure. How can there be any surprises if she's hearing it from the real you?

Off and Running

I've done a few things in my life of which I am not proud, but one of the worst was moving out on my girlfriend without letting her know.

The relationship was on the rocks, and there was no hope in sight. She took off one weekend with her girlfriends, and, upon her return, I was gone. It was all about me. I couldn't see beyond my own feelings or consider what it would be like for her to pick up the pieces on her own.

If you ever find yourself in that kind of pressure cooker, be a man, not a mouse. Unless the woman is threatening you with bodily harm, don't run. Even if the verbal abuse seems to be more than you can handle, don't run. If you don't get my point, it is this: don't run.

I'm not saying that moving out isn't an option—I'm just saying that it's a decision you shouldn't make on your own. I don't know why I was so afraid to communicate my feelings to her, but I'm sure that if I could dedicate the next six months to therapy, I'd be able to come up with an answer.

I know I'm not the only guy who has ever run from a sticky situation. I believe most men get used to being on their own. Then, when a woman begins to cramp their style, men want to hurry back to their own private Idahos.

Not allowed. As I learned, running is unforgivable. If you were man enough to begin the relationship, stand tall and be man enough to end it appropriately.

On Air

The young girl's voice sounded as though she was no more than twenty years old; the on-air personality confirmed that she was actually nineteen. She went into full detail about her problem: Her boyfriend wanted to sleep with her, but because she didn't want to, she feared that he would end up sleeping with her best friend.

Many people these days, especially teenagers, are going on air to solve their personal problems. In the old days, that's what parents, friends or therapists were for, but technology has taken over, making the media into a virtual third parent.

Radio shows provide a safety net for such shy callers—if you disguise your voice and use a fake name, surely people won't be able to identify you. Unfortunately, your voice is as easy to identify as your name. Somewhere out there, someone is listening, and they might just know who you are.

I've listened to married women call in to talk to shock jocks, boasting about their great sex lives—with men other than their husbands, information you would probably think twice about telling even your closest friend. Why, then, tell it to the world?

No matter if you're on the radio, on television or in a chat room, do yourself a favor and keep your most intimate information to yourself. Telling juicy secrets on the air is tantamount to the worst kind of gossip...even if it's juicy gossip, no one really needs to know your darkest secrets.

If you are inclined to do so, make sure the person you're speaking to can really help you, as opposed to exposing you for good ratings. There are qualified on-air personalities; how much you decide to tell them is strictly up to you.

Melvin's doctor says he can't go within
ten feet of a donut shop.

One a Day

These days, waking up seems to be a chore for many working people; hence, breakfast becomes secondary. Even when some folks do eat breakfast, they only make time for coffee and donuts, which don't come close to supplying the nutrition your body needs.

Vitamins and minerals, often found in breakfast foods, should be an essential part of your daily routine, just like waking up and going to the bathroom.

Caffeine has already proven itself to be a killer, so skip the coffee and head for juice or water. If you're going to put something in your body, why not treat it to something good?

Take your pick: Vitamin A, found in cantaloupe and peaches, is good for your skin and helps reduce lung cancer; Vitamin B, found in animal products such as milk and cheese, helps the nervous system, muscles and heart; and Vitamin C, found in tomatoes and oranges, aids in the prevention and treatment of the common cold.

Your body needs many daily vitamins and minerals, so taking a multi-vitamin is a good way to go. I have friends who carry little plastic bags filled with vitamins that they take throughout the course of the day. This may work for them, but I'm lucky when I remember to take my one-a-day all-purpose multi. Some vitamins will upset a sensitive stomach if not taken with food, so try to grab a banana or a bowl of cereal if your tummy is easily upset.

Besides vitamins and minerals, you can choose from a long list of supplements, including antioxidants, amino acids, herbs and holistic alternatives. Consult a nutritionist or do some research on your own; if you have health insurance, your provider may already have a nutritionist that you can see for a minimal fee.

Whatever you do, give your body the nutrients it needs by taking at least one multi-vitamin a day and trying to eat a balanced diet.

Courteous Carl makes sure that everyone
on his block has a place to park.

One Car, Two Spaces

Right outside my apartment building, there is plenty of space to park two cars, but because people generally don't think about the needs of other drivers, one parked car usually takes up both spaces. Think of how much easier the entire driving and parking experience would be if everyone operated in a frame of mind that included the needs of others.

I don't know about other big cities, but in Los Angeles, parking spots are precious commodities. Therefore, when there are a few hundred people within a four-block radius who could desperately use that space, it's incredibly selfish to take up two spaces.

The problem is partially due to the lack of painted parking spaces. On a regular residential street, there are no defined lines, so drivers don't think about the size of the space. Instead, they're just happy they found a spot, and then park willy-nilly, seldom taking into consideration the parking needs of others.

At night, parking people become even more thoughtless. It's late, it's dark and they just want to get home to eat dinner. Funny how that works…there's a guy right behind you who wants to do the same! Because you didn't pull up the extra two feet, which would have allowed him to park, he's onto the next block looking for a space, his dinner getting cold.

We've all been in the situation when parking somewhere, anywhere, is all that's important. However, you must remember that what comes around goes around. If you try to accommodate other drivers, you'll have more empty parking spaces to look forward to down the road. We all need our space, so if you're only driving one car, please try to take up only one parking spot.

Only In My Dreams

It was a Tuesday morning at the office when I walked up to Barbara's desk to tell her the exciting news. Well, it was exciting for me, but I wasn't sure just how much to tell her. You see, I'd had a dream the night before, and Barbara was—how should I put this?—the star.

She wasn't married, and she wasn't seeing anyone on a serious basis. I guess the big question was: Do I tell her about my dream or not?

Prior to the dream, I'd had *a little* interest in Barbara, but Tuesday morning, she was the only thing on my mind. I decided to ask her out for a drink and see how things went.

I'm not saying that sleeping with her on the first date was the right thing to do, but we both knew what we were doing, and we did it. The fact that we'd both had a few drinks sped things up; in this case, gin and tonics helped make my dream come true. Of course, this led to the usual feeling of awkwardness around the office and a relationship that probably shouldn't have started in the first place.

If you're lucky enough to have your dreams interrupted by someone who works with you, it may not always be to your advantage to tell them. She might be easily insulted or might consider your tale to be harassment.

If you want to test the waters, tell her about your dream without giving away too much. If she responds with genuine curiosity, feed her a little more. If she wears a look of disgust, make up something quickly, such as, "It was a circus, and you were one of the clowns."

Interpret your dreams however you choose, but if you ever decide to act on one, be prepared that your dream may not turn out to be a wonderful reality.

Other's Misfortune

Think about all those times when you or your friends picked on the fat kid in class or the kid with four eyes. Fast forward to today, and ask yourself if that mentality has changed.

You bet it has, because most of us are carrying around a few extra pounds, as well as sporting some flashy bifocals.

Now that we're older, we seem to enjoy the misfortune of others on a grander scale. If the stock market tumbles, and we hear Bill Gates lost two-hundred million in one day, I'm sure many penny-pinchers would say he deserved it.

On a different scale, take two teams about to meet in the World Series. One starting pitcher sprains his thumb and is out for the series. It's easy to see why the opposing team's fans might rejoice, but it's never the right thing to do.

I don't care if it's Bill Gates or a ballplayer, it's never right to kick a man when he's down. If a person committed a crime, then he deserves to be punished, but why punish an individual who has done nothing wrong other than suffer from a little bad luck?

I'm sure plenty of your co-workers, friends and neighbors have been down on their luck. Let's say the guy down the block is about to lose his house because he can't pay the mortgage. You only know this because other people in the neighborhood are making light of it. Instead of joining in their debauchery, pay that guy a visit and see if there's anything you can do to help. It's a small world out there, and sometimes a good friend is hard to find.

Out of the Closet

It's a fact: People form opinions based on the clothes you wear. Nothing is ever going to change that fact…people would probably judge what you were wearing even if you wore no clothes at all. Instead of thoughts like, "He really needs to update his wardrobe," they might think, "He really needs to shave his back."

People make judgments about our appearances. There's no way around it. You can rebel, keeping a shaggy face and sloppy clothes, but isn't it easier to dress a little spiffily and make a good impression?

Fortunately, our society has provided us with a great selection of style, and the object is to fit in without sticking out too much. Get a feel for what others are wearing in your environment and always be aware of any dress code. If the head of your company wears Armani, and you're in the mailroom, find a happy medium, but don't start competing with the big cheese. If the CEO prefers wearing Hawaiian shirts around the office, I would suggest holding off on wearing a tie.

I'm not interested in making a fashion statement, but I do try to look respectable at work. If I had more money, my philosophy might differ, but for now I'm happy to be wearing clothes that aren't dirty, outdated or clashing.

We always hear that women want men with a sense of humor, but women also want men with confidence, and nothing makes a man shine more than a great appearance. Save your money until you have enough to invest in the greatest commodity of all—yourself.

"My parents and I have an
agreement. I come home once a month
and they get to see me.

Parental Visit

They helped put you through school, bought you your first car and even sent you money after you moved out—so why is it so difficult to visit your folks every now and then?

I guess you lived with them for so long that spacing on your obligatory parental visits is almost like breaking away. Regardless, take a little time each week to visit your mom and dad. If they live too far away, pick up the phone. If one of your parents is deceased, that's even more of a reason to spend a little time with the only parent you have left.

I used to avoid visiting my father. I was ashamed because I hadn't pursued a successful business career like he wanted. What I failed to realize was that he didn't measure success by the amount of money I made, but by the amount of time I spent with him. Of course, my sister had to point this out to me, but I eventually learned the lesson.

Spending quality time with your parents doesn't mean running in, grabbing a meal and hitting the road. Quality time can be anything from sitting on the couch and talking, helping them around the house with chores or just watching a ballgame with your old man.

I was by my father's side when he was in for surgery and stayed with him at home during his recovery, which meant more to him than anything I'd ever done for him. It also made me realize that you can never spend too much time with your parents. Let's face it—you only have one set of parents, so enjoy them while they're still around.

148

Plenty of Prep

It doesn't matter if it's a first date or a job interview—the more you prepare, the greater the results will be.

Let's take a date, for example. So many considerations go into the date before you even pick her up: You need to make sure you have a clean house, clean clothes and a nice overall appearance. You might need a haircut before your date or even a car wash, too! Maybe you've been working in your backyard and have crescents of dirt underneath your nails...don't you want to scrape them clean before taking the hand of the babe you've got lined up?

It's important to take a good, long look at yourself before you get to her front door. If you're planning to go back to your place, don't rule out maid service to get your home looking presentable.

The same time and effort should go into job interviews. You can never look too good for the person you're hoping will employ you. If you grab lunch before the meeting, you may want to brush and floss so no miscellaneous food particles become the focus of your interview. Polish your shoes, press your shirt and make sure your outfit flows in a subtle way. Go over your resume so you're ready to answer any questions about yourself and your work history.

Let's say you already have the job and you're preparing for a meeting filled with heavy hitters. Think in terms of how you liked to feel before your college finals, knowing you were going to get an "A" before you even sat down because you prepared for the exam.

With a little effort and the right amount of preparation, you can get an "A" for the rest of your life, whether the exam is about dating, interviewing or presenting.

Power of the Wave

Unfortunately, there is a long list of ways you can make enemies while behind the wheel of a car. There's the obvious—cutting someone off or not allowing them to merge—but one of the most frustrating things you can do is fail to thank someone for being considerate. I am referring, of course, to the "wave."

We have all experienced this scenario: A line of cars is backed up at a stoplight, so it's impossible for you to exit the restaurant parking lot. The light turns green, and the line of cars begins to creep forward, slowly. Just when you thought nobody would let you in, another driver gives you the signal to merge, and you're on your way. It's like they stopped their world to let you get in front of them.

The only problem is that you didn't smile and you didn't wave, so it's like someone held the door open for you and you walked through without acknowledging his kindness, which, as we learned in an earlier chapter, is taboo.

There's really no excuse for this behavior. You can eat hamburgers and French fries in the car while you talk on your cell phone and listen to the radio, but you can't wave your hand to say thank-you? I don't get it.

I'm not advocating that you need to start singing show tunes to everyone who waves you in, but you do need to wave thank-you. At times I'll even lower the window and wave outside just to make sure they see it. It's important to be not only a defensive driver, but a considerate one, too.

Split screen saved their marriage.

Quality Time

My wife goes to school, and I work close to sixty hours a week. On the weekend, she usually has to study, so I use that time to write and do chores around the house. It would not be out of the ordinary to live our lives under the same roof and maybe see each other a few times a week, which means we don't make enough time for loving, touching or squeezing.

Regardless of your demanding schedules, it's important to take time out and spend a little quality time with your partner. Go see a movie, lie in bed or take a walk, but do something that will strengthen your love bond. Quality time can be spent at a bar, slamming back a few cold ones, or in one of the many coffee shops probably within walking distance of your home.

I like to give my gal a hug every now and then and look into her eyes as I hold her. The week is so filled with stress that nothing brings me back to her heart more quickly than looking in her eyes. Okay, there is *one* other thing, but if you can't make time to take off your clothes and get jiggy with it, simply putting your arms around her wouldn't hurt.

Give her a kiss before you leave for work and a warm embrace upon your return. Show her you love her; don't just tell her occasionally and hope she remembers.

This is your soul mate we're talking about, so no matter how serious those little fires that you spent your week putting out, nothing compares to your biggest priority: the woman in your heart.

Religion at Your Door

It's Sunday morning at nine a.m. The doorbell rings. For a moment, you just think it's your head pounding from the night before. Another ring of the doorbell, and you're out of bed, down the hall and out to the front door.

You look and feel like hell frozen over, but you open the door anyway. Standing in front of you are a man and woman who look like they starch their socks. No orange juice, pancakes or Publisher's Clearinghouse...the only thing they want to give you is another chance to avoid burning in hell.

Long before the age of the Internet, religious fanatics have been finding the way to your front door, trying to convert you. Here are my top ten excuses for those who come a-knockin':

10. Can you come back tomorrow? A guy is supposed to be here any minute to sell me magazines.

9. I'm Jewish, but I eat pork.

8. I'm house sitting...for Satan.

7. I'm not interested, but my girlfriend is...and I'm about to go dig her up.

6. This is a bad time—we're in the middle of dinner, but we can't get the chicken to stop moving.

5. I'm not interested in your religion, but do you have something to stop this jock itch?

4. I can't—I'm in the witness protection program.

3. I'd like to see your credentials so I can check them with God.

2. I can't right now—I just converted through an infomercial!

1. I would, but the last time I converted, I didn't see my family for two years.

Religion is no laughing matter, but people who bother you without permission are ripe for mocking. Seriously, be kind if you can, but always be careful for whom you open the door.

155

"When I was your age, I had a ton of women, or maybe it was just one woman who weighed a ton."

Respect Your Elders on the Bus

Whether it's holding a door open, helping them off with a jacket, or giving up your seat on a crowded bus, always help a senior citizen whenever possible.

Many selfish people in this world would never consider giving up their seat for an elderly person. That doesn't mean you have to follow that behavior pattern. In fact, you can't even blame those individuals because they may have never learned manners or proper etiquette. All you can do is lead by example and hope your fellow passengers learn to practice what you teach.

If you take it upon yourself to set an example, there's a good chance that others will follow. However, please understand that just because a person is over a certain age, it doesn't mean they can't stand on their own. Don't be insulting and insist the elder person sits if he says he's fine standing. You should be able to figure out their needs by their appearance...if that person seems too old or too sick to be standing, offer up your seat. If you see an obvious sign, such as a walker or a cane, it should send a signal that the person needs relief.

If you're with someone who needs to sit down, but no are seats available, you can certainly ask someone kindly if he would relinquish his seat to your elder friend.

Growing older is a bummer for everyone, especially those who suffer from any number of age-related ailments, such as Alzheimer's, Parkinson's or heart disease. Although life gets tougher for elderly people, it can get a little easier when the youth of this country treat them with respect.

Save the Mess for Last

Barbara went to house sit for a friend of hers. When she entered the kitchen, she was surprised to see that her friend had already gone grocery shopping.

"How kind," she thought, as she went to empty the bags resting on the floor. Upon closer inspection, however, she discovered that the bags were empty and not from a grocery store, but a Chinese restaurant.

"How odd," she thought, until she saw the open containers on the kitchen counter: beef teriyaki, won ton soup, vegetable chow mien and more bits of fried rice on the counter than there were in the box.

The mess, combined with the smell of day-old food, was enough to elucidate Barbara about what kind of person her friend really was—inconsiderate and a major slob.

If you want to live in your own filth, it's entirely up to you, but if you ask someone to look after your home while you're gone, you'd better make sure your place is spotless.

If your house sitter is also looking after your dog, give Rover a bath so your guest isn't overwhelmed by the stink of dog. Leave enough food and water in an easy accessible place; don't expect your sitter to haul her cookies to the store for Rover's haute cuisine.

If you were sloppy enough to leave out the remains of last night's dinner, who knows what may be lurking inside the other rooms? An unflushed toilet? Dirty towels? Expired underwear strewn across your bedroom floor?

Don't turn your home into the set of a horror movie. Clean it thoroughly and stock it with the necessary supplies. Your house sitter isn't your servant; she's a friend doing a favor, even if you're paying her.

Say Anything

Sometimes it's better to keep a tight lip rather than say something inappropriate, insulting or hurtful. On the other hand, it's sometimes better to speak up rather than not say anything at all.

If you keep your mouth shut too often, you may miss meeting the woman of your dreams. On a smaller scale, if you ask your waiter for a recommendation, you might change your dinner order to something infinitely more interesting than your standard Chow Fun.

When we first talked about keeping a tight lip, it was directed at meeting women and not letting too much out of the bag too soon. However, think about how many women you could meet if you didn't play the shy guy and just spoke up. Say anything—that is, anything that makes sense and sounds somewhat intelligent.

Good things to say: "Hello" or "I couldn't help but notice you" or "Nice outfit." Telling a woman you couldn't help noticing her might be a lot to get out if you're fumbling with your thoughts, so do whatever works best for you…as long as you do something.

You might want to write down a few of those opening lines and tuck them into your sleeve for your next outing. Practice them while you're driving or just taking a walk. If you rehearse, your sincere gambits will come to you more naturally when that unexpected "meeting" next occurs.

Say It with a Shirt

I was in a department store last weekend and saw, pushing his baby in a stroller, a man wearing a T-shirt with the "F" word emblazoned on the front—three times.

I've heard of freedom of speech, but was he really trying to exert his First Amendment rights, or was he just being a complete jackass? The last time I checked, adults were supposed to be setting good examples for their children, not acting as a billboard advertising profanity.

I don't know if this particular individual was planning to retire the shirt before his baby could read—perhaps he was thinking he'd give it to his child as a hand-me-down? Either way, his shirt was grossly inappropriate, especially for a public place. He may not care if his children are exposed to profanity, but other parents in the vicinity might not feel the same.

Plenty of T-shirts push the envelope on decency, but why contribute to the social ineptitude of our society with that kind of rubbish? Today's youth have it tough enough—they certainly don't need any more encouragement, let alone unspoken approval to say bad words. After all, if they've seen it on a shirt worn by an adult, it must be okay!

A marijuana leaf is also a popular symbol on t-shirts, and clearly expresses that the owner of the shirt loves his pot. Great. If you want to get high, do it at home. If you want others to know you get high, leave a message on your answering machine, but don't wear your reefer-clad shirt in a public place where parents will need to explain it to their children.

If you're an adult, start taking responsibility for not only what you say, but also what you wear.

Bill has found a way to enjoy
breakfast again.

Scrape, Squirt, Swirl, Crunch!

When dessert arrived, my dinner date and I devoured the chocolate soufflé like it was the last treat on earth. The raspberry sauce on the side was also delicious. What came next, however, was anything but…

Once we'd eaten the soufflé, "Noisy Nancy" felt the need to scrape every ounce of sauce off the plate, regardless of what kind of sound she produced. I ended my meal with dignity; it's too bad Nancy didn't do the same.

In retrospect, the entire meal was a disaster. Nancy refreshed her iced tea with a lemon wedge that squirted me in the eye. Go ahead and laugh…it's only funny until someone gets hurt. If she only would have covered the lemon with her hand, it would have been better for me and my vision.

Unfortunately, she didn't stop there. Even though the waiter provided a straw and a spoon, Nancy used her index finger to mix the fresh lemon into her drink. The highlight, of course, was when she licked her finger after swirling it in her tea.

Once she finished her glass of iced tea, Nancy kept sucking the straw…she must have wanted everyone to know she was out of tea, or perhaps she was trying to get her dollar's worth and suck up every last drop. I guess Nancy didn't know that the restaurant offered free refills.

My physical attraction for this woman reached an all-time low when she filled her mouth with ice-cubes and proceeded to let the restaurant know she wasn't leaving until she won a gold medal in the ice-crunching competition.

If you're in public, do your best not to make a spectacle of yourself over something as simple as a meal. No one wants to hear what you're eating or drinking.

Screening Calls

Caller ID is one of the pure joys of modern technology. With the increasing volume of telemarketing calls that inundate us these days, I don't know how anyone could choose not to screen phone calls.

For every ten calls, at least five are from telemarketers. When they call, my Caller ID displays "Unknown Name" and "Unknown Number." Of course, I don't answer the phone if I don't know if who's calling, so most thwarted telemarketers hang up before the outgoing message has even ended.

However, when a call comes in from someone you know and the machine has already picked up, it's decision time. Will you or won't you take the call?

If you don't take the call immediately, then you have to call the person back. If it's a long-distance call, then you can save time and money by taking the call. However, if you know it's going to be a long discussion, and you're on your way out the door, you have no choice but to run.

People sometimes feel the need to make excuses about why they're screening their phone calls. Why bother? It's nobody's business but yours. Don't feel like you have to say anything except a warm "hello." If your friend or family member doesn't have Caller ID, and it bothers them to always reach your machine, politely say this is the way it has to be until they decide to identify themselves when they call.

She's the One

On their first date, my father knew he would marry my mother. I don't know if that happens any more, and if it does, I haven't heard too many instances of it. However, there comes a time when most men realize that their girlfriend is the woman with whom they want to spend the rest of their life.

Within my small circle of friends, the shortest amount of time from when a couple met to when they got married was four months. I can't quote the longest because I have too many friends who are still competing for that title.

When that moment of truth arrives, it may not be at a time when there is peace within the relationship. For example, it's possible the two of you had a fight and called it quits. Then, one day, you realize you can't live without her, but it's too late because she's long gone.

Many will argue that you gave it your best shot, so move on, but I beg to differ. I believe that men make a ton of mistakes for a million different reasons. If you want her back that badly, give it everything you've got—and understand that it will probably be the last chance you get with her.

A woman gives her heart; a man usually waits for a bigger, better deal. As a guy, you have to realize that if you're with someone you'd love to see at breakfast for the rest of your life, then you've already won the lottery.

Your woman is everything…and then some. When the moment comes when you just know she's also the one you want to marry, accept it for what it is—your heart telling you not to let this one get away.

Smudge City

Your good friend just bought a brand-new car and can't wait to show it to you. He drives up and parks the car, and you can't help but be impressed. After giving it the once over, you press your hands up against the window to check out the interior. Congratulations! Your pal's new car now has your stamp of approval!

Fingerprints, smudges, call them what you want, but be very careful where you place your bare hands—especially if you're leaning on a new car. A few smudges might not seem like that big of a deal to you, but now your buddy has to clean the window where you touched it, a situation that could easily have been avoided with a little consideration on your part.

Imagine you're at your friend's house, watching the football game with a few of the boys. It's a relaxed atmosphere, so you kick off your shoes and plop them onto his glass coffee table. God only knows where your feet have been, but it looks like you just might create a new dance step with all the footprints you're leaving on your pal's table. If you're going to put your feet up, takes your shoes off and keep your socks on. Don't make smelly, sweaty footprints.

Window-shopping is a popular activity in stores and jewelry stores, where panes of glass become a conglomerate of bacteria, germ central, where other window-shoppers have placed their hands. Be on the safe side and window shop without actually touching the window.

In fact, try to avoid any contact with glass that will leave a mark saying you've been there. Let them remember you by your sparkling personality, not the smudges you left behind.

Supermarket Savvy

Some people walk into supermarkets and eat various food items for which they never pay. Guess what? That's called stealing! If the deli or bakery offers up free samples, that's one thing. Grazing at the salad bar or idly snacking on individually wrapped candy is another. Eat what you pay for, and pay for what you eat.

Most supermarkets have bins containing fresh candy and pastries. Prongs are usually provided, so you don't have to use your hands. Unfortunately, supermarkets could have set shovels outside each bin, and shoppers would still dig in with their bare hands. Needless to say, prodding the bagels is disgusting and unhygienic, so in the name of Mr. Onion, Egg and Poppy seed, please keep your hands to yourself.

Most markets have shopping-cart bins with large signs explaining that if you leave your cart elsewhere, you will damage private property. Furthermore, these shopping-cart corrals are strategically placed throughout the parking lot, so you don't have to walk all the way back to the market to return the cart...because the storeowners know how hard it is to walk those extra twenty yards. It's ironic how many aisles you walk up and down while you're shopping, but once you're outside, every extra step seems painful.

Do yourself a favor and shop like a respectable human being. Whether you're inside or outside the market, it's time to set an example while grocery shopping. Hopefully, others will follow your lead.

Talking with a Toothbrush

Most people brush their teeth at least twice a day. During each dental workout, it's probably better for you to concentrate on brushing and nothing else.

Toothpaste triggers brainwaves in my wife's head; she has a bad habit of asking questions with her mouth full of toothpaste. I don't care how cute your wife or girlfriend is...there is nothing less attractive than a face full of foaming fluoride.

If she can't do it, neither can you. I worry about men a little more because they tend to become caught up in exciting events, such as the arrival of their wife's Victoria Secret catalogue or a football game. It's the end of the third quarter, and that mouth should have been rinsed out closer to halftime.

Don't get me wrong, I highly recommend brushing your teeth in front of the television. Everyone should spend a little more time brushing their teeth, as opposed to rushing through the process. On any given day, compare how much time you spend eating junk food opposed to the time you spend taking care of the thirty-two little bones that allow you to enjoy junk food—your teeth.

On the flip side, you don't want to brush for too long because of the deterioration excessive brushing may cause your gums. That's why many dentists recommend brushing with a soft brush.

I'm sure these same dental professionals would also tell you to avoid talking with your mouth full of toothpaste, but since I'm here, I'll tell you for them. You have plenty of time during the day to carry on a conversation. Dedicate the time you brush your teeth to observing a moment of silence.

Taster's Choice

I have a group of friends who gets together a few times each year and goes out for dinner, usually to celebrate a birthday or some other special occasion.

Without fail, there will be dish swapping. It works like this: Debbie orders prime rib, Steve orders fish, Carla orders oysters, and Paul orders pasta. When the meals arrive, everyone starts to second-guess their menu selections because everyone else's dish looks better.

Before you know it, plates are being passed around, forks are plowing into other people's food, and everyone is getting a taste of everything. Then, as the atmosphere begins to settle down, a strange silence creeps over the table. That's when the other six people at the table discover that everyone contributed to the feast except me.

Let them think what they want. I am not—and I repeat, *not*—into dish swapping. If I order it, then I eat it. I don't need anyone's help, and I don't need to taste food off any other plate but mine. Heck, I'm just glad I have an appetite after witnessing this carnage every year.

Of course, that's just me. I have discovered that food swapping is one reason people like to go out for dinner. However, the only set of silverware that is going into my food and my mouth is my own. If you are stuck somewhere in the middle, here's an option: cut off a portion of your meal and drop it onto another plate, rather than having the natives attack what is rightfully yours. It will send a signal that you are trying to keep peace amongst the tribe.

The bottom line is, it's your meal, so you do whatever makes you happy. If that's sharing your dish, so be it. If not, don't feel bad about being hygienic and eating what you ordered.

Trash Talk

The only thing worse than being woken up in the morning by a loud trash truck is looking at the empty trashcans your neighbor leaves on the street for the next three days.

It's truly amazing that anyone can get up and go to work for eight hours, but can't find the time to bring in their empty bins. It only takes a moment, and it improves the visual quality of the neighborhood for everyone.

I used to wheel the emptied cans up my errant neighbor's driveway as a kind gesture, but it got to a point where I think they expected me to do it on a weekly basis. Well, I need to be paid if I'm going to do someone else's dirty work, so I threw in the towel. Unfortunately, not much changed.

As a rule of thumb, bring in your trashcans the same day as the trash pick-up. If you aren't going to be home, kindly ask a friend or neighbor to bring them in for you; surely you can reciprocate some day.

At the same time, if your trash pick-up is on Friday, don't put out your cans until at least Thursday noon. Burglars scope out neighborhoods looking for signs, such as bins that are out too early in the week, knowing quite well it can mean that nobody's home.

Don't make yourself a target. If you are leaving town, ask someone to take out your bins and bring them in after they're emptied. Most of the neighbors I know enjoy helping out each other. It's the ones who don't who usually leave their homes looking a little trashy.

Turned Down and Let Down

I recently interviewed for a job that seemed to be a wonderful opportunity. The set of interviews went very well, and they offered me the job.

I don't think they expected me to turn down their offer, and I'm sure they didn't expect to receive a gift basket to thank them for considering me. On the other hand, I expected at least a phone call to say "thank you" for the gift basket, a phone call that never came.

As an individual working hard to exhibit proper etiquette, it's sometimes difficult when you extend yourself, only to be ignored by the other party. It feels like not being congratulated for a job well done...thanks are important, but requiring them can feel petty. After all, if you know in your heart that you've done something good, then it shouldn't matter what anyone else has to say.

I guess this interview was an unusual situation because the gift basket I sent wasn't cheap, and I don't have a lot of money to throw around on unnoticed gestures. It was not the reason I turned down the job, but their failure to offer a simple "thanks" certainly made me feel better about my decision.

On a smaller scale, perhaps you send a Christmas gift to a friend who never tells you he received it. Instead of leaving you to wonder if your friend received the gift or if the postal service lost it, there is an easy way to remedy this situation: your friend could send you a thank-you card in return.

Birthday cards are a little more personal, so take a moment out of your day to say "thank you" to someone who took a moment to think of you on your natal day.

Regardless of the occasion, don't let someone's failure to recognize your act of kindness make you stop doing what you do best—being kind. Just because they behaved badly, it doesn't mean that you have to do the same.

Under the Influence

Life can be difficult. Don't make things worse by allowing others to influence your decision-making abilities.

A close friend was dating a girl for several months before he invited her to lunch with his guy pals. A total of six people were at the table, including two of my buddy's co-workers. Later that afternoon, his two colleagues told him he could do much better when it came to women. One week later, he was back on the market looking for someone new.

Seeking advice is a good thing, as long the advice you receive is in your best interest, not someone else's. In my friend's case, he received advice from two guys who were single and wanted him to stay that way. Was their advice in his best interest? Hardly.

There comes a time where you have to make decisions on your own. It's you who has to live with them, not anyone else. If you're constantly receiving bad advice from people you consider friends, perhaps you should drop them down one notch into a new category, called "acquaintances." I don't care how close you are to a particular individual; the final answer should always come from you.

Advice from a family member can be a different story. I was about to buy my first home when I asked my father to inspect the house before I signed on the dotted line. He must have picked out a dozen problems that I didn't see, saving me from spending my money on what would have become a money pit.

If you need help making a tough decision, go with a friend or a family member you can trust. If nobody is around, go with your next best ally, your heart.

Unwanted Gifts

A friend of mine has a bad record when it comes to giving gifts. It's not that he doesn't give—it's *what* he gives.

"Lousy-Gift Larry," as I like to call him, has never bought anyone a gift for as long as I can remember. He gives the free merchandise department stores give away when you buy a bottle of cologne. For your birthday, you might receive from Larry a bar of soap, a travel bag or perhaps a small kit filled with shampoo and after-shave.

For my birthday, Larry gave me a coffee cup emblazoned with the name and address of a local real estate agent, as well as a lovely photograph of the woman. I told Larry that the least he could do was to put a few quarters inside the mug so I could do laundry!

To add insult to injury, he gift-wrapped the coffee mug, thinking, no doubt, that it might enhance the value. I'm not ungrateful, but why bother gift-wrapping something like that? Give an unwanted promotional gift to a friend for the sake of giving, but don't give it to a friend for his birthday.

It really is the thought that counts. Take two minutes out of your day to consider what kind of gift your friend might enjoy receiving. If money is an issue, there are plenty of nice gifts that don't cost a lot, such as a candle, a frame, a bottle of wine or even a plant.

The basic rule of gift giving is to use your brain, meaning you should buy something your friend can use. There's no need to give a bad gift—a card would have been better than the lousy gift Larry gave me.

Note: I don't believe a thank-you card is necessary if you receive a gift like I did from Larry, but you should send a thank-you for just about anything else.

Waiting Is the Hardest Part

Marsha had a few people over for dinner to celebrate her promotion at work. She spent the day cooking and was looking forward to serving her friends a new rack of lamb recipe she had discovered. Her guests arrived on time, she served the food, and, when she was about to sit down to join them, she discovered that one of her guests had almost finished the helping she had just served.

Although Marsha was gracious, taking the guest's rudeness as a compliment, deep down, she wondered where "Bonehead Bob" had learned his manners.

It doesn't matter if you're dinning at Marsha's house or a fine restaurant—wait for everyone to get their food before you dive into yours. If the person who hasn't been served insists that you start—especially if you're eating something hot, like soup—go ahead and start, but pace yourself so you're not done with your meal before the other person has a chance to start his.

Patience is a virtue, whether you're dining at Marsha's or just waiting on someone to return a phone call. She'll call you back when she has a chance; if she doesn't, you should take that as a clear indication that she isn't interested.

Perhaps you're restless over a job you really want. Everyone has a tendency to jump the gun and become too pushy, as opposed to letting things fall into place and following up as appropriate. Take a deep breath and know that you've done everything you can up to this point. Waiting is the hardest part, but you will be pleased that you did.

Since Bart took the gun off his rack and replaced it with Sparky's leash, he seems to be doing better with the ladies.

Walk the Dog

If a dog is man's best friend, and my target audience is men, then it makes sense that I would impress upon you the importance of walking your dog.

Outside of watching you open a fresh can of Alpo, a walk is a dog's favorite activity. Get out of the house and take your dog for a walk. He'll love it, and it's a great exercise for you, as well.

You would think picking up after your dog would be a no-brainer, right? Wrong. If picking up after your dog is so simple, why am I always greeted with fresh droppings every time I inspect my front lawn? The answer: People—not dogs—are often lazy and inconsiderate.

Make sure your dog is on a leash when you walk him. If a person is walking in your direction, pull your dog aside so he won't bother the oncoming pedestrian. Nine times out of ten, strangers will want to play with your pooch, but there's always that individual who doesn't like dogs. They may even have a fear of dogs because of an incident in which they were once attacked. Be considerate—pull your dog aside until the passerby passes.

The same holds true for encounters with other dogs. If both dogs are wagging their tails like there's no tomorrow, chances are good they'll lick, smell and play with each other. However, too many dogs are unpredictable, so don't take any chances unless you ask the dog's owner if their companion is friendly.

Of course, let's not forget the most important element of walking your dog—they are chick magnets. The cuter the dog, the more babes you'll be sure to attract—which should be reason enough to take man's best friend for a stroll.

190

Water Resistant

I try to get to the gym as often as possible. Unfortunately, while at the gym, I witness endless instances of water abuse. In the men's locker room alone, I'll often see men shaving over sinks with the water running. If it normally takes a few minutes to shave and the water is gushing the whole time, that's a heck of a lot of water to waste! Everyone likes a close shave, but you shouldn't have to drain a dam to get that clean comfortable look.

It makes me uneasy watching all that water go to waste. Believe it or not, I've walked up and asked several gentlemen to be more conscientious of the water they waste.

People become advocates when the feel strongly enough about something. I feel so strongly enough about water conservation that I'll go out of my way to prevent it, no matter where I am.

For example, if I'm walking my dogs and see a broken sprinkler in the neighborhood, I'll do everything in my power to alert the homeowner. If I'm in a restaurant, using the bathroom, and notice a leaky pipe, I'll notify the manager, citing a hefty water bill as the best reason for him to make the repair.

You may believe in keeping your nose out of somebody else's business, but when it comes to wasting water, it's everyone's business. Water is more than just a precious commodity; it's essential to our body composition. Heed those 1970s environmental warnings and do your best to conserve water every chance you get. Conserve water whenever you can, and spread the word so others will begin to conserve, too.

"Per your request, we have removed the
TVs from each room, bolted the beds to
the floor and replaced each mirror
with aluminum foil. Enjoy your stay!"

Weekend with the Boys

Las Vegas, Nevada. Bachelor Party. Ten guys, one suite and enough booze to furnish the wedding reception. It's a little difficult to maintain proper etiquette when you're in this type of atmosphere, but don't let your manners completely go to pot. Hang your clothes, put down the toilet seat and tip your escort— not necessarily in that order!

In all seriousness, someone has to set an example, and there's a good chance that someone might be you. Beer cans will be crushed, potato chips will crumble, and somebody's underwear will end up on the balcony—and that's just in the first hour. Someone must monitor the insanity and clean up when the mess threatens to overtake the room.

Take heed: Just because you have manners, it doesn't mean you have to become the token maid. Take care of yourself like you usually do, and try to maintain some sort of normality, but don't become the janitorial service for the entire party. Lead by example.

If trash starts to accumulate in every place except inside the trashcan, point out the nearest waste receptacle. If you order room service, call housekeeping when you've finished your the meal so your tray doesn't sit around for the remainder of the weekend. Unless told otherwise, the maid has to clean every morning, so the boys need to make sure their belongings are not scattered everywhere.

The single most important thing for you to remember is to have a good time. If you're close with one or two guys who look like they could use some etiquette advice, pull them aside if the opportunity arises, but don't act like you're trying to be their mother.

The bottom line is that they have to learn somewhere, and, after reading this book, you'll practically be an expert. A weekend with a bunch of slobs is actually a nice way to appreciate how far you've come toward better etiquette.

What Comes Around...?

People who don't believe in karma probably write off the unknown as coincidence or just bad timing: If they don't hold a door open for a person, and then walk into a door the very next day, chances are they won't put two and two together and realize their own rudeness earned them a bonk on the nose.

Karma is real. What comes around does go around. I don't want to get too deep and explain why good people go to heaven and bad people don't, but on a very simple level, those who treat others with respect and dignity can expect the same in return.

If a guy and a girl hook up and it doesn't work out, that doesn't make him a bad guy. However, if a guy tells a girl he loves her just to get her into bed, then his actions become questionable.

A close friend of mine went through women like they were cherries—he would chew them up and spit them out. Years later, he had a change of heart and began to look for a girl with whom he could get serious. On the rare occasion when he found someone he liked, she usually ended up treating him like dirt, a classic case of him getting a dose of his own medicine.

My friend is still alone and searching. I keep telling him the right woman is out there, but the "powers that be" will make her appear only after he has suffered three times as much as the women he dumped. I know it sounds harsh, but if you treat others poorly, you have to be ready to suffer similar consequences.

Don't let me be the judge...there's a power much greater than myself who decides who's good and bad. That power has a name: karma. Don't mess with it.

Who Invited Him?

I was having lunch with a buddy of mine, when a friend of his walked up and dove into our conversation. Ten minutes later, I was trying to finish my lunch, while this guy was still yapping away. I was tempted to buy him lunch, if only to keep his mouth occupied with something other than chatter.

I don't care whether it's a restaurant or a bowling alley, if you see an old friend who is with somebody else, say "hello," and then wrap it up quickly. Small amounts of chat are fine, as long as it doesn't turn into a sermon.

You have no idea what you might be interrupting—a job interview, an argument, a debate about higher powers or just two old friends who haven't seen each other for a while. It doesn't matter. Acknowledge your friend, and then get moving.

At the gym, I saw a personal trainer in the middle of a session with one of his clients. A third party walked up and asked the trainer for suggestions on how to lose the tire around his waist. The trainer politely mentioned that he would be happy to help, but that he was busy with a client at the moment. The third party huffed away, oblivious of the *faux pas* he just committed. After all, the trainer was on someone else's dime!

Time is a valuable commodity for everyone, so be aware when you interrupt someone else. If you respect other people's time, then they will be more likely to make plenty of time for you.

Yesterday's Water

Some people like to keep a fresh glass of water on their nightstand, so it's there whenever they need it. It may come in handy during the night, when they get thirsty, or even in the morning, when they wake up with a dry mouth.

While a glass of water might be convenient, that glass won't stay fresh for very long. Even if your brilliant mind tells you to cover the glass with a napkin, the water is still sitting there exposed to a slew of nasty things. Do yourself a favor and change the water, without fail, every single day.

Clean the glass once a week so you don't get Mr. Potato Head growing inside. Do the same with the glass you use to rinse your mouth after brushing. You know the one—the glass with the scummy layer at the bottom, where your fingers can't possibly reach. Furthermore, never allow your toothbrush to soak in water, which becomes a breeding ground for bacteria you wouldn't want in your mouth.

For those of you who do care, keep your bathroom accessories as clean as possible, and don't hesitate to buy yourself a new toothbrush every few months. For less than what it costs to buy a six-pack of beer, you can have brand new toothbrushes as often as you want.

We live in a society where people pierce their tongues, chew tobacco and smoke big, fat cigars, so I don't know if a dirty toothbrush would really affect these individuals. However, if you don't have any of these bad habits, then you don't want to acquire one nearly as nasty.

You Could Have Called First...

"You could have called first" has become a very common phrase uttered in relationships; unfortunately, it's never really used when things are going well.

If you have a date, but you're running late, don't even think about showing up without calling first. You're obviously interested in this girl, so you don't want her to think that you're inconsiderate *and* habitually late.

Maybe she's cooking you dinner. If an entire meal has been prepared on your behalf, one phone call is the least you can do to let her know you're running behind. Then, she can at least keep the food warm. Make sure to tell her your estimated time of arrival, and give her another call if that ETA changes.

What I'm saying should already be instilled in your head from all those years of phoning home to tell your mother you'd be late. You should have the same attitude when it comes to dating, and just think of how proud it will make your mom to know she's raised a punctual and considerate young man.

Even if you're past the stage of dating and have a wife, don't leave her hanging. Women spend a great deal of time and energy looking after their men, so if you're going to meet up with a friend after work for dinner, let your wife know.

Picking up the phone might seem basic, but I wouldn't be writing about it if the problem didn't exist with almost everyone I know. Remember, the telephone is your friend. Your wife will remain your *best* friend if you would simply pick up the phone.

Conclusion

The toughest part about jogging is putting on your shoes—it's all about taking the first step. The same holds true with learning proper etiquette.

The good news is that you may already have read the first installment of *Etiquette for the Average Joe;* now that you've completed *Volume II,* your shoes are on and you're off to the races!

Unfortunately, this race never ends because there is an endless amount of information to learn when it comes to having good manners and proper etiquette. However, you can hold your head high and claim a victory when you know in your heart that you are doing your very best to behave like a respectable gentleman, educated in the ways of proper etiquette.

I should give you fair warning: the third volume of *Etiquette for the Average Joe* is on the way. As good as you feel about the advances you've made, the next book will push you just a little further to better yourself.

I never think I've learned everything, and there's never an end to what I can teach. The truth is that I could go meet a friend for a drink and notice something that I've never seen before. That's why it's important for you, the reader, always to keep your mind open to areas upon which you can improve.

Perhaps, one day, you might even order flowers for your wife or girlfriend when it's not her birthday or your anniversary. This behavior, while not falling under any specific etiquette category, will certainly make you a better man. That's why we're here, isn't it?

When you get a chance, go to www.etiquettefortheaveragejoe.com, and bookmark it. I just want you to know that you can contact me whenever you have a question or concern. Don't think of me as an author, think of me as a friend. Long live good manners and proper etiquette!

About the Author

In November of 2003, the first volume of "Etiquette for the Average Joe" was released, and before he could say "Calgon take me away," Martin Stuart was touring the country making appearances on morning television talk shows and nationally syndicated radio programs. When not busy with his book promotion tours, Martin travels extensively to lecture at high-school, college, and corporate events.

When he's not on the go, Martin Stuart lives with his wife and two Dachshunds, they split their at home time between Southern California and British Columbia.

Aside from writing, Martin enjoys playing golf and collecting wine. His other passion is to attend the many sporting events and piano recitals in which his nieces and nephews participate.

Please write to Martin Stuart @ PO Box 5413, Playa Del Rey, CA 90296, or visit him at w w w . e t i q u e t t e f o r t h e a v e r a g e j o e . c o m . . . w h e r e you can also buy the book.